We Are Included!
The Métis People of Canada Realize Riel's Vision

John W. Friesen, Ph.D., D.Min., D.R.S.
Virginia Lyons Friesen, Ph.D.

Detselig Enterprises Ltd.
Calgary, Alberta

DETSELIG
ENTERPRISES LTD

We Are Included! The Métis People of Canada Realize Riel's Vision

Canadian Cataloguing in Publication Data

Friesen, John W.
  We are included! : the Métis people of Canada realize Riel's
vision / John W. Friesen, Virginia Lyons Friesen.

Includes bibliographical references and index.
ISBN 1-55059-272-6

  1. Métis. 2. Métis--Legal status, laws, etc. 3. Métis--History.
I. Friesen, Virginia Agnes Lyons, 1952- II. Title.
FC109.F75 2004   971.004'97   C2004-902428-0

Detselig Enterprises Ltd.
210, 1220 Kensington Road NW
Calgary, Alberta T2N 3P5

Phone: (403) 283-0900
Fax: (403) 283-6947
Email: temeron@telusplanet.net

www.temerondetselig.com

We acknowledge the support of the Government of Canada
through the Book Publishing Industry Development Program
(BPIDP) for our publishing program.

We also acknowledge the support of the
Alberta Foundation for the Arts for our
publishing program.

SAN 115-0324   Printed in Canada   ISBN 1-55059-272-6

*To Cheryl Gottselig
with sincere appreciation*

The Red River cart, an exclusive Métis invention, was made entirely of wood and the wheels were lubricated with fat renderings. A slow-moving wagontrain of a few hundred carts made loud shrieking noises that could be heard for miles as wooden wheels ground against wooden axles. Often called "half man and half cart," an individual cart carried nearly 500 kilograms (1 100 pounds) of meat. Pulled by huge oxen, Red River carts could float across rivers when they were forded.

Table of Contents

Introduction – Irrepressibility 11

One   Integrity 23

Two   Identity 41

Three   Ingenuity 51

Four   Initiator 73

Five   Images 97

Six   Inculcation 115

Seven   Intensification 137

Bibliography 147

Index 161

Our goal is to see Aboriginal children get a better start in life as a foundation for greater progress in acquiring the education and work-force skills needed to succeed. . . . To see Aboriginal Canadians participating fully in national life, on the basis of historic rights and agreements – with greater economic self-reliance, a better quality of life. . . . The Government will engage in other levels of government and Métis leadership on the place of the Métis in its policies.

– Speech from the Throne, Ottawa, Ontario, Government of Canada, February 2, 2004, page 10.

Batoche Church Rectory

Batoche Rectory Dining Room

Batoche Church Priest's Study

Batoche Church Rectory Kitchen

Caron Farm House, built in 1895 to replace
one destroyed by Middleton's troops

Preface

The Métis people of Canada are experiencing a coming of age, a new beginning. Weary of living below the poverty level, amid poor social conditions, and with minimal educational opportunities, for the last several decades their leaders have addressed these issues with an increasingly effective voice. Frustrated at having been ignored for so long by historians and government bureaucrats, they have fought hard to obtain what they deem to be their legal right—the right to status as Aboriginal people.

Their case has been won, thanks to the Supreme Court of Canada decision of September 19, 2003. Background to the event includes reference to two separate cases regarding Aboriginal rights. In 1993, a Métis hunter, Steve Powley and his son, Roddy, were arrested in southern Ontario for hunting moose without a license. They claimed they were members of the Métis Nation and were therefore acting within the parameters of their Aboriginal rights. It was this case that laid the groundwork for the supreme court's decision. The Powley's successfully argued that they had a constitutional right to hunt for food, without obtaining a provincial license and outside of provincial hunting seasons.

A second case of interest involved Ernest Blais, a Manitoba Métis who was also arrested for hunting without a permit. He too, claimed he was exercising his Aboriginal rights (*Alberta Native News,* April 13, 2003: 5). In a third case, in December, 1998, Ontario Judge Charles Vaillancourt acquitted a northern Ontario Métis charged with hunting without a license on the grounds that the Métis indeed possessed Aboriginal hunting rights. The judge stated that a Métis is an individual who says he or she is Métis and whose claim is accepted by other individuals whose Métis identity is not in question (*Calgary Herald,* January 9, 1999: H5). Even if

Judge Vaillancourt's interpretation of the law pertaining to Aboriginal rights is correct, however, the delineation of who is Métis will not be as easily applied. How many individuals who claim Métis affiliation will it take to determine if someone is entitled to Métis Aboriginal rights? Bloodlines will not necessarily be a factor in determining identify. In any event, the Métis people of Canada now have a toehold by which to proclaim their legal and cultural identity.

It may take some time before the Métis case for cultural integrity will be nationally accepted, but Métis researchers are hard at work. Recent literary efforts include collections of articles and papers such as those produced by the Gabriel Dumont Institute of Métis Studies and Applied Research in Saskatoon, Saskatchewan, and the Louis Riel Institute of the Manitoba Métis Federation in Winnipeg, Manitoba. A recent release is entitled, *Métis Legacy: A Métis Historiography an Annotated Bibliography* (2001), edited by Lawrence Barkwell, Leah Dorion and Darren Préfontaine. This 512 page volume contains an extensive accumulation of Métis material culture including the largest collection of previously unpublished articles. A tribute to Métis presence in Canada, the project was sponsored by twenty national organizations, most of them with Métis affiliations. Another recent book arguing the case for the Métis, edited by Jacqueline Peterson and Jennifer S. H. Brown, is entitled, *The New Peoples: Becoming Métis in North America* (University of Manitoba Press), shows encouraging signs of public interest by being made available in its fourth printing.

Louis Riel continues to fascinate and beguile North Americans as may be evidenced by the steady stream of writings about his life and career. These have recently been summarized by Alberta Braz in *The False Traitor: Louis Riel in Canadian Culture* (2003). Undoubtedly the enamor with Riel will aid the Métis cause and serve as a beacon to draw attention to more serious matters.

Until very recently, there were three dominating perspectives pertaining to Métis status in Canada. First, there were those who believed that the Métis should be regarded as a fullfledged Aboriginal community with all the rights pertaining to that status. Second, and for a long time there were individuals and groups who recognized the integrity of Métis culture as a unique society, but afforded it no legal recognition. Métis writers are currently trying to stitch together the various pieces of that cultural patchwork quilt. The basis for their endeavors is the fact that Canadian multicultural policy is definitely committed to the objective of recognizing and encouraging the development of the various cultural sectors that make up this nation. There is no reason why the Métis should not find a satisfying role in that milieu, although this option was not sufficiently recognized to satisfy the majority of Métis leaders. They did not believe that recognition of cultural uniqueness was enough to alleviate the negative conditions in which many Métis live.

The third option has been to ignore Métis pleas for justice and equality and simply continue to maintain the status quo. This stance may have worked in the short run, but it has not been particularly useful as a long range policy. Like their Status Indian peers, Métis political strength in Canada has been growing, to say nothing of population increases. As late as 1973 the average Native individual in Canada could expect to live 43 years while the average Canadian (including Natives), could expect to live 62 years. By 1995 these figures rose so that Native males could expect to live to be 69 compared with 75 for Canadian males as a whole. Native women could expect to live to be 76 compared with 82 years for Canadian women as whole (Frideres and Gadacz, 2001: 66-67). If the present trend continues, for example, by the year 2020, one-third of Saskatchewan's population will be Native people, including Status and nonStatus Indians and Métis.

Knowledge is power, and Aboriginal political strength is matched by educational attainments as Native youth in larger numbers continue to graduate from high school and pursue post-secondary education. Native students only began to attend post-secondary institutions in significant numbers in the 1970s. By 1981 the Canadian census revealed that two percent of the Native population held university degrees compared with 8.1 percent of the NonNative population. In 1996, when the report of the Royal Commission on Aboriginal People was made public, it indicated that 4.2 percent of Aboriginal people held university degrees compared with 15.5 percent of nonAboriginals. Twenty-one percent of

Aboriginal individuals had completed a college certificate compared with 25.5 percent of nonAboriginals.

In the years following, these numbers have increased. For example, the number of Status Indians and Inuit enrolled in post-secondary institutions almost doubled between 1988/89 and 1997/98, rising from 15 572 to 27 100. Against these developments it becomes obvious that the Native people of Canada cannot be ignored. The Métis quest for recognition and justice is part of the larger campaign of the Canadian Indigenous community and must not be swept under the rug. Hopefully, this book will provide sufficient information to aid readers in understanding Métis efforts in this regard.

This book was inspired by our many visits to Batoche and Duck Lake, Saskatchewan, as well as inspections of other important Métis sites such as Cutknife, Fort Pitt, Frenchman Butte, Frog Lake, Loon Lake and Winnipeg. Louis Riel's imprint is on all those places, but most significantly in the hearts of those who consider themselves his followers, partakers of his dream of a new nation.

We would like to thank our friends at Batoche and Duck Lake for their kindness in sharing the story of Riel and his people with us through the years. If this book in any way assists them in realizing their objective it will have been more than worth the effort in preparing it.

John W. Friesen
Virginia Lyons Friesen
The University of Calgary

Introduction
Irrepressibility

The biggest mistake the Dominion government ever made was in stopping Louis Riel. – diary entry by R. B. Bennett, Prime Minister of Canada, July 24, 1886. (Colombo, 1987: 327)

Today the Métis make hardly any impression on the Canadian consciousness. Riel, however, continues to fascinate us. – Thomas R. Berger (1982: 26).

The Métis have played a central role in the history and development of Canada, especially Western Canada. Formal recognition in . . . the Constitution Act, 1982, has placed the Métis in a strategically important position to pursue their individual and collective interests in the changing character of Canadian society. – Lance Roberts, Susanne von Below, and Mathias Bos. (2001: 193)

The word Métis in French means mixed or cross-over. This definition may therefore be interpreted to suggest that historically the Métis were a bridge between two nations, local Aboriginals and incoming Europeans. The Métis were a unique race born for a new country, born to frame a new national identity. The merger of the two cultural communities occurred shortly after the first European explorers and fur traders arrived and negotiated marital unions with women of Indigenous background. The result was that a new subgroup originated, namely people who had both Aboriginal and European heredity. As successive generations have unfolded, however, it is highly likely that members of the first generation were probably the only ones to equally represent the two bloodlines.

Sadly, the "bridge" people have received little formal recognition over the centuries that they have held their unique status. Their descendants have too often occupied the lower rungs of Canada's socioeconomic ladder, and formal recognition of their identity by the federal government did not occur until 1972. Today things are slowly changing as the Métis gain political strength and

11

public support. Their growing population is also a factor. There are currently 292 310 people in Canada who identify themselves as Métis, an increase of 40 percent over the last five years. Over the past century the Canadian Aboriginal population grew by 22 percent, while the Métis population grew by 43 percent.

Interestingly, the largest Canadian Métis population is in Alberta, not Manitoba, the province which Louis Riel helped bring into being. Alberta's Métis population stands at 66 055 while Manitoba's Métis population is 56 795. Two-thirds of the Métis in Canada live in urban areas, and the rest live in rural areas. Winnipeg, Manitoba, is home to 31 395 Métis, Edmonton, Alberta, to 21 065 Métis, and Vancouver, British Columbia, to 12 505 Métis. Over 7 000 Métis live on reserves, a number that has doubled over the past five years.

Social descriptors of the Métis differ significantly from those of the nonNative population. These statistics are not particularly enviable. For example, 23 percent of the Métis people changed residences during 2002, while only 14 percent of the general population did so. Nearly one-third of the Métis population is under the age of 14 compared with 19 percent of the general public. Only 4 percent of Métis are over the age of 65 compared with 13 percent of nonAboriginals in Canada (Statistics Canada, 2003).

Despite obvious social and economic differences between Métis and nonMétis, which characterize the former as occupying a less advantageous status, there is evidence to suggest that the Métis are gaining a stronghold in the Canadian cultural milieu. They are now the fastest growing and youngest sector of population in the country.

Beginnings

Canada, in fact, requires only to be known in order to be great.
J. Castell Hopkins, editor, (1998). Introduction, Vol. 1, *Canada: An Encyclopedia of the Country.* (Colombo, 1987: 49)

Although Canada is a very young nation, relatively-speaking, the country has gone through significant changes since it earned its formal status as an independent nation in 1867. Obviously no one really knows when this great land was first occupied since the oral history of the First Peoples is not always specific as to time and place. We do know that the territory which became Canada was occupied by many quite divergent First Nations for centuries before the arrival of the Europeans. For many generations Canadian historians virtually ignored any happenings before European emigration, partially because of a lack of familiarity with or appreciation for the oral tradition.

On April 20, 1534, Jacques Cartier's ship sailed to the east coast of the new world where he met "wild and savage folk" who clothed themselves in the furs of animals and wore their hair tied up on top of their heads like a handful of twisted hay (Ray, 2002: 2). His contact with Aboriginal people was preceded by Leif Ericsson in 1497 and John Cabot (Giovanni Caboto) in 1520. Neither of these explorers provided much information about First Nations cultures since their primary motivation for coming to the New World was economic. If pushed, like their contemporaries, they probably would have described the Aboriginals as uncivilized peoples whose cultures and values were obstacles to economic and social progress. These explorers were not schooled in the art of ethnological appreciation nor were they particularly attuned to studying alternate lifestyles.

Not many years ago, Métis historian, Olive Dickason, set the record straight with two significant books: *The Myth of the Savage and The Beginnings of the French Colonialism in the Americas* (1984), and *Canada's First Nations: A History of Founding Peoples from Earliest Times* (1993). Dickason filled in the blanks about the life and times of the Indigenous peoples before European arrival, and defended their cultural lifestyle. Although commonly described by European newcomers as "savages" or "uncivilized people," Dickason pointed out that many of the atrocities committed by European invaders easily outranked anything the Aboriginal peoples had done to one another in times of war. Dickason's analysis did not go unnoticed by her academic peers, and shortly thereafter all published works of history in Canada began to acknowledge the cultural contributions of First Nations to this country.

On another positive note, when formal negotiations became part of interaction at the time of first contact, the First Nations were in fact regarded as political equals, and governors of separate states. This perspective was maintained to the process of treaty-signing (Patterson, 1972: 1). When the economic benefits of the fur trade began to decline, however, the invaders wearied of the arrangement and initiated a colonial system aimed at diminishing the rights of the Indigenous peoples. The process of colonization took many forms, chief of which was education. The initial thrust was to operate day schools as a means of assimilating Indian children, but efforts soon turned towards the establishment of residential schools. In this arrangement children were wrest from their parents and made subject to an educational program with two definitive prongs. The first was to acquaint children with European religion and values and the second was to try to convince them that the lifestyles of their ancestors were uncivilized and, in fact, heathen ways.

Cultural Variations

The lifestyles of the original North American nations encountered by the European newcomers differed significantly from that which they left behind. The Europeans perceived that the cultural makeup of local residents was basically the same across the continent and did not take time to discover the error of this assumption. They were also unprepared to discover the diversity of resident language groups nor the depth of Aboriginal spirituality (Friesen, 2000).

One of the chief differences between the world-views of the incoming Europeans and the First Nations had to do with values. The Indigenous people based their way of life on knowledge systems rather than tools solely considered essential to survival. Landspace was abundant, population was sparse, and there was plenty of game to go around. The people took time to enjoy life without feeling any pressure from the effects of industrialization. The Europeans, on the other hand, came to North America to obtain furs, conquer the settled peoples, colonize them, and expand their foreign kingdoms.

The Europeans were in for some linguistic and cultural surprises. The First Nations of Canada spoke at least fifty different languages according to the first classification of languages undertaken by John Wesley Powell in 1891. Powell classified North American First Nations' languages into a total of 58 stocks. Later he modified this classification to 51 stocks, and in 1921, Edward Sapir reduced the list to six stocks broken down to 11 language groups.

The western coastline, later known as the British Columbia coast, was perhaps home to the most linguistically-diverse area on the continent. Seventeen languages from five different language stocks, were spoken. To the north were the Haida and Tsimshian (the latter divided into three language groups), as well as the Tlingit. The central groups originated from Wakashan stock, and included the Kwakiutl (now known as Kwakwaka'wakw) who spoke three languages, the Nootka (now known as Nuu-chah-nulth) who spoke two languages, and the Bella Coola (now known as Kuxalk), were a northern enclave of Salish speakers. Further south were six more language groups, collectively labelled "Coastal Salish." Four of the five stocks occurred only on the west coast and all five are unique in Canada to British Columbia.

Métis Origins

The origin of Métis culture is specifically tied to the fur trade dating back to the 17th century when French Canadian voyageurs and Hudson's Bay employees began trading in the area. Their marital unions with local Cree and Ojibway women produced children labelled "Natives, Mixed bloods," and "Halfbreeds" by the Hudson's Bay Company. The latter term, which is biologically impossible after the first generation, gradually acquired a pejorative connotation (Payment, 1990: 20). It has been a long struggle for individuals of Métis background to squelch the negative propaganda surrounding their origins and convince Canadians to acknowledge their legitimate place in the country's history.

The Riel Story

The historical record shows that on November 16, 1885, Louis David Riel was hung, charged with six counts of felony-treason under the 1352 English Statute of Treasons. Scarcely four months had transpired from the date of his trial on July 20, hardly a proud moment in Canadian history for "due process," but not unlike many other trials of the time. The jury deliberated only 90 minutes before bringing in a guilty verdict, then requested that the court show mercy. The judge ignored the plea and sentenced Riel to hang.

A little more than a hundred years after Louis Riel's death, on March 27, 1992, Alberta Attorney General Ken Rostad, on behalf of the Métis Association of Alberta, requested that the Government of Canada pardon Louis Riel. A month earlier the federal government passed a motion recognizing Riel's contribution to Canada whom the Métis people view as a founding father of the nation (*Calgary Herald,* Friday, March 27, 1992: A13).

It helps to adopt a long range perspective of history when try-ing to synthesize the two events of 1885 and 1992. Time changes things, and often people are not prepared for the dimensions of altered ways. International happenings are a case in point. Who would have suspected a few years ago that the Berlin wall would come down, the Soviet Union would dissolve, apartheid would begin to crumble in South Africa, and the United States would ignore a United Nations' resolution and declare war on Iraq?

In relation to Louis Riel's career, critics might ponder how an individual's life and work could be viewed so differently within such a short span of time? Placed in the context of the story of humankind, a century is a relatively brief passage of time. At the time of Riel's execution the decision to hang him left many of his Métis followers disillusioned, upset and angry. The government, however, insisted that he had acted with malice against the nation (Braz, 2003). He was labelled a traitor who had attempted by force and arms to subvert and destroy the nation's constitution and therefore had to be put to death. In a less than revered volume, Siggins (1994) argued that Riel was eliminated because he was holding up western Canadian development. Riel's secretary, William Henry Jackson, held Prime Minister John A. Macdonald responsible for Riel's failed mission, because the latter had first negotiated with the Hudson's Bay Company and completely ignored the rights of the Métis to their homeland (Smith, 1981: 13).

Conversely, a campaign to pardon Riel will also upset some Canadians, particularly those who interpret Canadian history from Anglo or dominant societal perspective. Professor Thomas Flanagan, a Riel scholar at the University of Calgary, stands firmly behind the observation that the Métis war of 1885 did not originate because of Métis grievances, but because of Riel's own sense of reli-gious destiny and his own grievances (*Alberta Report,* December 5,

1983: 36). As a result, any attempt to re-write history to exonerate Riel should be met with strong resistance.

Despite Flanagan's misgivings, nationalistic movements are frequently propelled by charismatic leaders who arise from within the ranks of the community in question. Louis Riel had strong ancestral linkages within the Métis community. He was born at St. Boniface on October 22, 1844, to a family who could trace their ancestry back to the closing days of the 17th century and the founder of their line – Jean Baptiste Reel of France, who immigrated from Ireland. Riel's mother, Julie Lagimodiére, was the daughter of the first white woman to make her home in the Canadian west (Anderson, 1974). His father, Louis Riel Sr. was mostly French, though there were claims that his mother's family had Chipewyan bloodlines (Purich, 1988, 47). This would mean that Louis Riel Jr. was one-eighth Indian, but born and raised in a distinctly French cultural configuration. It is commonly believed that the Métis People originated as the offspring of liaisons between French male fur traders and Woodland Cree and Ojibway females. Children born from other liaisons such as Scotch and Aboriginal were usually labelled halfbreeds (Dobbin, 1981: 18-19). On this basis it is necessary to make note of Louis Riel's unique personal journey which led him to the front lines of the Métis movement.

Riel's Role

The story, in brief, begins with the career of Louis Riel Sr., a successful miller who encouraged his son to take up formal studies. As a result, for ten years, young Riel studied humanities, law, and the classics, and even considered a call to the church ministry. Eventually he took up employment with a law firm and thus met many active and aspiring politicians including Wilfred Laurier who later became Canada's Prime Minister. Several incidents influenced Riel to abandon interest in his studies and he subsequently spent some time in Métis settlements in southern Manitoba. His search to find collegiality for his mission paid off, and he soon found himself at the forefront of the Métis cause.

Ancestral bloodlines are not necessarily a stronghold for breeding patriotic or nationalistic leadership causes as the case of Peter Lougheed, a former Premier of Alberta, illustrates. Lougheed can boast of having the same percentage of Native ancestry as Riel (Lougheed's grandmother was Métis), but he has rarely been a champion for the Native cause. He was a strong opponent of the campaign to entrench Native self-government in the new constitution at the first such conference in 1982, although in a surprise move in 1985, he proposed a measure of self-government for the Métis of Alberta in response to a call for a revision of the Métis Betterment Act (Purich, 1988). At that time the Alberta Legislation unanimously passed a resolution calling for a transfer of ownership of settlement lands from the government control to Métis settlements themselves. The resolution included constitutional protection for the transfer (Purich, 1988: 150).

Aside from this surprising stance, Canadian history shows that Lougheed was a hard-line opponent to the inclusion of Aboriginal rights in the Canadian Constitution as demonstrated in his behavior at the 1984 and 1985 constitutional conferences on Aboriginal rights. While Louis Riel undoubtedly found a measure of personal satisfaction in advocating the Métis cause, Lougheed, whatever his reasons, ferreted out what he thought to be legitimate claims on the part of the Métis from the "non-legitimate" claims of Native peoples generally. Bloodlines then, in no way comprise reliable grounds for interpreting individual behavior.

Negative Foundation

The roots of the Métis story, quite bluntly, are bathed in racism. The Métis interpretation is that the story began in Europe in the sixteenth century when business leaders needed cheap labor to help them glean profits in the new world. Since the Native people were expert hunters and trappers, the fruits of their labors were envied and sought after. To keep them in their place so that exploitation of their wares and labors might continue, the European explorers manufactured a philosophy of Native inferiority backed by theological and educational foundations (Adams, 1975: 5). This imperialistic campaign continued without interruption even though neither the conversion nor education of Aboriginal people reached any remarkable proportions.

The schemes devised to accomplish the "educating and civilizing" of the Indian were diverse, including day schools and industrial schools, placing Native children in the homes of model nonNative families, and even transporting them to Europe to live with families over there via an adopt-a-student program. None of these schemes were very successful and around 1890 the residential school plan was formulated. This format required that First Nations children were to be taken from their parents and educated for ten months of the year in boarding schools run by religious denominations (Brookes, 1991). Children were often expected to serve as domestic servants to school staff. They were also forbidden to speak their Native languages, and were required to attend regular chapel services. They were not allowed to sit with nonAboriginal neighborhood children when the latter were allowed to attend movies at school (Friesen, 1983).

The Native peoples of Canada have been the target of a two-pronged cultural attack since the European invasion of the 17th century. One dimension of the crusade concentrated on the perpetual slavery of the Aboriginals which would auger well in the drive to maintain cheap labor. Dominating military rule enforced this arrangement while religion and schooling supplemented it. The end result was a defeatist attitude on the part of the First Nations who eventually saw themselves as fit only for menial labor (Adams, 1975: 4). The other thrust of the crusade was to civilize the Aboriginals in an effort to help them abandon their traditional ways and incorporate alternative European values. Many nonNative observers were shocked when they finally realized that neither thrust was effective. Despite this failure, efforts to assimilate Native people into the dominant society through educational means continues to this day in a virtually unaltered form since it was first incepted many generations ago (Friesen and Friesen, 2002: 87-88).

The effects of a continual onslaught against Native cultures has had severe repercussions in the Métis community. The Métis community has borne the cross of scorn from both Status Aboriginals (those Natives legally recognized by the Indian Act), and nonAboriginals with a measure of dignity. Their cultural pride has been maintained through various means devised by their leaders. Perhaps being the target of perpetual disdain has aided them the most, and with the possibility that Louis Riel's contribution to

Canada will finally be seen in its true light, Métis pride is undoubt-edly at a new high.

A Note of Hope

The esteem with which the Métis regarded Louis Riel during his military efforts on their behalf was not an isolated gesture. When his quickly-arranged death sentence was announced, peti-tions requesting clemency poured into Ottawa from all parts of Canada, Britain, and the United States. French Quebecers were indignant. Hopefully the weight of these objections will be viewed as constituting sufficient grounds for a re-examination of the role of this unique individual (Bowsfield, 1971: 145). As time has shown, that historic concern has finally been awarded a second chance in the possible exoneration of Louis Riel.

Regardless of what happens to Louis Riel's reputation, the real-ity is that a movement is underway to persuade Canadians to acknowledge the validity of a distinct Métis culture. Peterson and Brown (2001: 6-7) argue that mixed-blood peoples with Aboriginal ancestral bloodlines from all over North America are becoming cognizant of common heritages and values. The increasing tenden-cy of groups in the United States and Canada to use the word Métis as a symbol of a collective identity is a strong indicator that the quest is sincere. Since 1965 Métis associations and federations have been founded in every Canadian province as well as in the States of Michigan, Minnesota, North Dakota, Montana, and Washington. The objective of Métis nationhood is definitely finding stronger support and unity.

A Note on Terminology

There are a variety of terms to choose from in writing about the original occupants of this continent. One can choose from Aboriginal Peoples, AmerIndians, First Nations, First Peoples, Indians, Indigenous Peoples, Native Peoples, and North American Indians. Recently a colleague suggested that the First Peoples in Canada be called "PreCanadians!" There are writers, Native and nonNative, who prefer a particular usage to the exclusion of all the others. Currently the Government of the United States, and writers in that country, prefer the term "Indian," while Canadians are opt-ing for "First Nations, Indigenous People," or "Aboriginals."

Despite arguments to the contrary, a variety of these usages will be employed in the ensuing pages, partly to relieve monotony in delivery, and partially because it is difficult to know which usage might be appropriate in any given context. In addition, words to describe the First Peoples will be capitalized as a means of emphasizing the literary legitimacy of writing about the AmerIndians, in the same way that identities of other nationalities are capitalized.

1
Integrity

The half-breeds [Métis] as a race never considered themselves as humble hangers-on to the white population, but were proud of their blood and their deeds. (Stanley, 1960: 10)

The diversity of Alberta's . . . Indian tribes was first augmented by the arrival of French, British, and later American traders, *and by the emergence of a new people,* the Métis, offspring of the intermixing of fur traders and Native peoples. (Palmer & Palmer, 1985: ix, italics ours).

The purpose of this book is to outline the history of Métis claims for legal recognition of their Aboriginal Status. Métis writers argue that for too long Canadians have had to rely on the established historical record in learning about their people, but that record has concentrated too much on the plight of the Métis People of Canada and neglected their historical role and cultural contributions. Recent happenings on the Aboriginal scene, and particularly in the Métis community, have provided a strong motivation to reexamine the evidence behind Métis claims and emphasize the more positive aspects of their case.

Academically, an undertaking of this kind would normally necessitate a close scrutiny of primary sources such as archival records, government documents, and diaries or correspondence pertaining to the main characters of the story. Rather than adopt this approach, however, a much less stringent scholarly tack will be adopted here. This admission may cause historians to cringe a little, but there are some reasons (good ones, we hope), for choosing this route. The discussion will offer an analysis of the better-known works on Louis Riel and the Métis people from the perspective of evaluating the question, "What if the Métis are correct; what if they really deserve to be regarded as a culturally-distinct people, even a Charter Nation?" Further, what are the political and cultural implications of such a reality? Minimally, it must be conceded that the

Métis *should* be perceived and officially recognized as a unique and separate entity in the kaleidoscope of Canadian multiculturalism to a greater degree than has been the case in the past. It is a Métis hope that they be regarded as a fast-growing, confident, independent, distinct, and direction-oriented cultural community.

A New Mandate

Although the supreme court decision of September 19, 2003 dealt with only one of two specific cases regarding Métis rights, the ramifications of the decision are far-reaching. Trevor Gladue, President of the Métis Nation of Alberta suggests that the action of the court implies that Métis health, education, and welfare may eventually be under federal jurisdiction. Ralph Goodale, federal interlocutor for Métis and nonStatus Indians agrees (*Alberta Native News*, October, 2003: 5).

The supreme court decision also stipulates a working definition of Métis as anyone who can prove a connection to a stable continuous Métis community. More importantly, perhaps, is the issue of land claims which the Métis will presumably be able to pursue. Before the court decision was handed down, Tony Belcourt, Minister of Litigation for the Métis National Council and President of the Métis Nation of Ontario, described it as the most important event affecting the Métis of Canada since the trial of Louis Riel (*Alberta Native News*, March, 2003: 10). The court decision is final, of course, but it can only have legal implications. Together the Métis and their fellow Canadians will have to come to grips with the nature and reality of Métis identity. Certainly the rapid Métis population growth will increasingly become a vital factor in these deliberations.

To many observers the argument that the Métis ought to be regarded as an Aboriginal people has been fraught with complexities. Contrary arguments have been quite powerful. In the first instance, no Métis were in Canada when the first informal treaties were made between European explorers and resident First Nations. As everyone knows, they were born of such unions. Second, if bloodlines are to be a factor in determining whether or not the Métis are to be recognized as Indigenous peoples, the case seems even weaker. It is safe to say that most Métis people in

Canada have stronger European bloodlines than Aboriginal. The Alberta Métis Association once met this challenge by decreeing that anyone with at least one quarter of Indian blood would be eligible to join their organization.

Following bloodlines as a means of establishing cultural identity is not a particularly fruitful avenue to pursue. The Supreme Court of Canada has chosen a different route, enabled by several important factors. These include recognition of significant customs, traditions, and practices that have not been extinguished by colonial powers and which are currently and have been practiced for a reasonably continuous period. The court further recognized that Aboriginal rights are those that do not have a major impact on nonAboriginal people or on fundamental provincial and federal governments. Such rights include customs, traditions, and practices that are necessary for the maintenance and development of Aboriginal societies (Supreme Court of Canada Court Case File No. C28533).

Culturally, the Métis have worked very hard in recent years to prove they historically developed a separate lifestyle, quite different than that of either Europeans or First Peoples. Their cultural contributions are gradually becoming recognizable, including stories about their former annual buffalo hunt, use of the Michif language, invention of the Red River cart, the Métis jig, arts, music, unique items of attire, and other elements. The communities they developed at Red River were distinct from those around them; they were neither European nor Aboriginal in style or format. The fact that the Métis generally adhered to the Roman Catholic religion (Dusenberry, 2001: 122), having adopted their faith from the father's side of the family, indicates that claim to having been raised in traditional Aboriginal spirituality would be a bit of a reach. Until recently neither the Roman Catholic Church nor Protestant denominations regarded Aboriginal spirituality as on par with European-derived forms of theology. Like other tribal societies around the world (Knudtson and Suzuki, 1992), Indigenous elders often point out that spirituality traditionally formed the very foundation of their cultural systems (Friesen, 2000), and this was certainly not the case with European-derived religions. Religion aside, there are a convincing number of factors that support the Métis contention that their cultural configuration should occupy a rightful place in Canada's multicultural mosaic.

A primary political difference between Métis and Status Aboriginals has been the matter of jurisdiction. For years the federal government has maintained obligations towards the latter group while the provinces were responsible for ministering to Métis needs. The federal government originally dealt with Western Canadian Métis as Aboriginal people and, ironically, is still dealing with the Métis in the Yukon and Northwest Territories as Aboriginals. The federal government does so on the basis that the northern Métis can base their claims on "national rights" rather than Aboriginal rights (Gaffney, Gould, and Semple, 1984: 19). Whether or not the Métis have national rights was not for the supreme court to determine; rather, the question was, do the Métis have Aboriginal rights or were those rights extinguished through adherence to treaty or receipt of land or scrip? What about those Métis to the north in the valleys of the Peace and Athabasca Rivers whose descendants demanded scrip rather than treaty status at the Treaty Eight signings in 1899? (Foster, 1983: 79). Did these happenings in any way set a precedence for those Métis in other parts of Canada who were not party to either treaty or scrip? In the final analysis, the Supreme Court of Canada examined the evidence, heard arguments, and made a decision. It will now be up to Canadians to validate the decision of the highest court in the land.

Complexities of the Quest

The foundation of the Métis political and cultural reawakening began as an offshoot of a First Nations campaign for greater recognition of their cultural, political, and legal rights in the 1960s (Shore, 2001: 78). The fact that the Métis piggy-backed on a First Nations initiated effort raised questions for some about the validity of Métis claims. True, in the last two decades the Métis amassed considerable evidence that supported their argument for cultural distinctiveness, but it did not necessarily make the case that they should be entitled to the same rights as Status or Treaty Indians. The promotion of Métis history, beliefs and folkways, and language overwhelmingly substantiated their case for cultural uniqueness (as it does for other ethnic minorities in Canada), but it did not necessarily place them in the same legal category as that of the First Peoples. The decision of the Supreme Court of Canada was the final word on the matter, and all that remains now is to operationalize it.

Before the 1960s the word "Métis" was virtually unknown in parts of Canada and the United States, despite the fact that many mixed blood people lived in those localities. When the civil rights movement in the United States became a public issue in the 1960s a simultaneous endeavor was underway in Canada to recognize the multicultural makeup of the country and respect the heritage and cultural lifestyles of all ethnocultural groups. Aboriginals mounted the same bandwagon and began an earnest attempt to gain government attention for their own concerns.

Riding in on the coat-tails of these efforts, Métis leaders began to agitate for recognition of their unique place in the nation's cultural and political milieu. This offensive is still underway, propelled by the efforts of many gifted public speakers and writers of Métis extraction. One of the challenges of the campaign is the disunity, dissension, and ambivalence within Métis ranks. This disunity has a long history. When they first invaded North America, it was the objective of the French to build one strong nation by cementing relations with local tribes through intermarriage (Dickason, 2001: 27). This objective was scuttled by the British takeover who had an entirely different imperialist view. Children born of interracial marriages were thus ignored and downtrodden and stripped of individual and cultural dignity. The scene was set for resistance. When it did occur, under Louis Riel's leadership, it did not represent the interests of mixed bloods across the land. It was only in the Canadian far northwest that conditions allowed for the development of a new nation which was ultimately destined to collide with the objectives of the new confederation.

Métis origins in Canada are regionally diverse. Some biracial families, for example, once founded fur trading companies and grew and flourished and as a result, separate mixed blood communities sprang up in various locations across the country. By 1815 there was ample evidence of a 150 year alliance between men of the fur trade and Aboriginal women (Peterson, 2001: 62-63). By the late 1820s, a population of ten to fifteen thousand residents of Métis communities could be identified in the Great Lakes region, but they did not become unified as a separate unit in Canadian life. When Riel later initiated his campaign for a new nation, eastern Canadian Métis were not even aware of it. Other Métis communities in Ontario, Montana, and even in Alberta were too preoccupied with daily matters and earning a living to hatch a unified national plan for Métis identity.

When news of Riel's endeavors spread across the nation, reactions among Canadians varied, even though most Métis sympathized with the cause. Despite this, Riel's plan to have the Canadian government recognize the new nation essentially lay dormant for more than a half century. Instead feelings of hopelessness and ambivalence prevailed, supported by government inaction and public disinterest. Thus when the Métis renaissance movement of the 1960s strode onto the stage it was difficult to unify their various constituencies. A myriad of Aboriginal, nonStatus and Métis organizations sprang into being, some of them quite at odds with one another about methods of procedure. This left Métis leaders with the difficult task of trying to unify the various factions and perspectives into a whole. That task, it appears, is still ongoing. The Métis do not have a history of cultural or philosophical synthesis; neither do they have a long record of either strenuous or successful political endeavor. The campaign to united their people so they will speak with one voice and do so successfully will be fraught with tremendous difficulty. If it works, they will still have to win the hearts of the Canadian people to their cause.

Perspective

This book offers a distinctly western Canadian bias, as will no doubt be caught by reviewers, but that perspective has been set upon without apology. True, the descendants of Louis Riel's "New Nation" currently reside in all ten provinces and both territories, and the first mixed marital unions between French and Aboriginals occurred further east. Until recently, however, most historians wrote as though such unions never existed (Dickason, 2001: 20), and the Métis in the east were unaware they were to become part of that identity. The origin and primary beginning of Métis culture per se occurred in Manitoba, thanks to the efforts of Louis Riel and his peers, and later shifted to the North West Territories which, at that time included the present provinces of Saskatchewan and

Alberta. This historical reality is the primary emphasis in this writing and the happenings in that area form the foundation of the underlying thesis.

The concept of recognizing Métis society as distinct is not new, of course, for Métis leaders have long been arguing their case. Some Métis take the position that at one time they as a people enjoyed territorial independence and socioeconomic interdependence with the rest of Canadian society as a culturally vibrant and separate viable society (Daniels, 1979: 4). Métis domicile in Canada involves a considerable passage of time as the durations of nations go on the international scale, and the Métis can point proudly to numerous inclusions of the actions of their people in the national historical record. That record includes reference to a fairly well-defined land-space for separate Métis communities, the adoption of a flag (three actually), the markings of a unique provisional government charter, and ample mention in the Canadian record by a variety of respected sources (including government documents), both recognizing and validating their presence as a distinct society (Daniels, 1979: 9). In addition, a few decades ago the Métis were finally officially recognized by the nation's federal government, and their representatives have been active participants in subsequent constitutional talks. Against this backdrop it would seem that the Métis case had considerable strength. Obviously, the Supreme Court of Canada recognized that.

The Argument for Distinctiveness

When the story of human civilizations is scanned, it is entirely possible to get a fair picture of what the biblical prophet, Isaiah, had in mind when he described nationhood as a rather insignificant entity in the cosmic scene of things:

> Behold, the nations are like a drop from a bucket, and are accounted as the dust on the scales; behold he takes up the isles like fine dust. . . . All nations before him are as nothing; and they are counted to him less than nothing, and vanity. (Isaiah 40:15, 17, King James Version)

There are undoubtedly a few recently-formed nations in the world (in Africa, for example), would admit to the tentativeness of their status, and they would probably be quite reluctant to concede a higher degree of validity to the status of more established nations. It is true that nations come and go in the scheme of things, but endurance over time is a fairly solid criterion on which to base cultural validity. The most valued format for determining or validating nationhood today seems to be a majority vote by the United Nations Assembly unhindered by a veto from a superior power. The Métis may not yet have fulfilled that criterion, but their long Canadian record certainly is supportive of their stance.

The Dictionary of Sociology and Related Sciences (Fairchild, 1964: 201) defines the word "nation" as a community of people who have their own political structure and territorial establishment. The definition allows that a nation may exist without separate political identity or self-control or even without the harmonious consensus of its constituents. The definition concludes with the corollary point that a true nation is probably the most stable and coherent large-scale human group yet produced by social evolution.

Nationalism, which is a logical derivation of nationhood, however, is a surprisingly recent phenomenon, dating back to the late eighteenth century. According to House (1992), the definition of nationhood was generated in part from shared print languages. When it became possible to print and produce low-cost printed matter, many speakers of the vernacular became readers for the first time. Certain languages or dialects and vocabularies became fixed, for example, the "King's English," which was then standardized and propagated from a central source. The message was usually one of unity and identity. For the first time geographically scattered people could conceptualize a community of which they were a part, stretching beyond themselves and their immediate villages, and even across time (Anderson, 1983).

When the historic situation of the Métis is analyzed against this definition it becomes apparent that many of the implied criteria for nationhood have been in place for a long time. Under the leadership of Louis Riel, the Métis claimed a specific territory and developed a very clear set of political structures. The fact that the Province of Manitoba originated as a result of Métis ingenuity sets the groundwork for the argument that they historically claimed a specific political identity and developed a workable, albeit short-lived form of self-control or self-government. What is more important is that they developed a high degree of homogeneity among themselves, quite different from the clashing immigrant minorities who were placed by chance in the same territory and who eyed each other with envy and jealousy. The Métis developed a sense of community, an orientation to consensus, and a respect for the accumulated wisdom of past generations.

The concept of nationhood conveys a myriad of implications about inter-relationships involving countries, regions, nations, and cultures. At one of the extremes, nationhood may become a religion in the sense that the concept itself may even become doctrinal, for example, the existence of the nation may come to represent the highest ideal of life. After World War I, a sense of nationalism developed in the form of anti-imperialism, as in Africa, the Middle East, Southeast Asia, and, most recently, the former Soviet Union and eastern Europe. Modern Nationalists invoke strong populist sentiments, a language of state, a nationalist ideology, mass media, education, and all the instruments of official nationalism turned against the mother country (House, 1992). Nationhood participation may involve organization, rituals and a specialized leadership or even "priesthood," and arouse an emotional self-consecration of the individual to the nation's systems of values. The relentless nineteenth century western expansion of Canada and the United States was justified by a nationalist belief in a manifest destiny; it was believed that the invading European nations had the right to take over the Aboriginals who lived on this continent (Appelbaum and Chambliss, 1995: 71).

Métis history is replete with references to the religious or spiritual dimension. Consider the visions of Louis Riel, for example. According to some of his biographers he was more than the average visionary (Stanley, 1963; Bowsfield, 1971; Flanagan, 1979a). Some social scientists have observed that human societies may even have such effect on individuals that their personality characteristics will resemble a commonality. Anthropologist Ruth Benedict (1934), for example, categorized Indigenous cultures according to personality types. She perceived the Haida of British Columbia to be of a Dionysian (aggressive) type because of their inclinations to value a highly-motivated lifestyle. Benedict labelled the southwest Pueblo Aboriginals as Apollonian (or peaceful)

Indians because they were more relaxed about life and indulged in afternoon naps.

Benedict's research engendered a degree of controversy over the decades since it was originated, particularly the tendency to overlook individual variations in clinching the orientation to identify common characteristics in a given nation (Sargent, 1949; Young, 1944). Most theorists today hold the view that the earlier years of socialization are the most important in forming common personality characteristics (Barnouw, 1979: 368), but there are also theorists who marshall evidence against the view that the early childhood years are singularly crucial in human psychological development during the formative years (Morgan, 1975; Clarke and Clarke, 1976).

Riel undoubtedly drew his visionary tendencies from his Roman Catholic faith, rather than from Aboriginal spirituality, since he was probably quite unacquainted with the latter. His time in a Roman Catholic seminary strongly reinforced his perceived mission and helped couch it in affiliated religious terms.

Cultural Indicators

The concept of culture is also relevant to this discussion if it may be allowed that the Métis can justly claim uniqueness in their cultural lifestyle. Culture is often defined as the social heritage of a nation or society. Each generation passes on to its offspring the design for living that it acquired from its forbears, and thus that generation is relieved of the necessity for reworking the solutions to innumerable recurring problems. Culture is also defined as the way members of a group of people think and believe and live, the tools they make, and the way they do things (Braidwood, 1955: 27; Friesen and Boberg, 1990: 120).

In another sense cultural variation is one of the ways in which observers can tell one group of people from another. Each cultural format represents a society's solutions to problems. Each generation of a society faces a number of identical problems simply because they share certain fundamental characteristics which require constant attention, that is, food, shelter, physical sustenance, personal identity, and security. There is some variation in the ways that different societies meet these challenges and this can affect the composition of the cultures which they formulate as a result. For example, some cultural configurations manifest a much higher degree of emphasis on cosmic elements than others do, and the range of religions, philosophies, legends, myths, folktales within systems vary greatly as a result (DeFleur, D'Antonio, and Defleur, 1973: 98; Friesen, 1995: 20). These variations are helpful in delineating differences in cultural patterns and often aid in providing an understanding of the importance of symbols in any given configuration. However, regardless of the manifest nature of these differences, in either physical or metaphysical forms, they must not distract from the greater underlying truth of basic human commonality.

Some critics argue that cultural determinists go too far in delineating culture as the most significant factor in shaping human thought and behavior. They point out that the human species has developed an impressive bag of tricks called culture, to control, modify, and indeed create an important part of the environment. Culture should not be seen as all-important, however, because it cannot be divorced from either ecology or genetics. All three influences are intertwined, and sway, impose on, and limit one another. Culture grows out of biological evolution and responds to multiple environmental forces. It also shapes ecology and therefore the biological evolution of the human race. Nothing is gained then, by trying to maintain a categorical distinction between nature and nurture (van den Berghe, 1981: 6). There is ample evidence to indicate that by the time Louis Riel assumed a leadership position among his people, he was responding as a member of a distinct minority, not representative of any specific First Nation.

In broader terms it is quite appealing to appreciate the Métis case for historical validity and cultural uniqueness. A catalogue of criteria to substantiate their claims would have to include mention of these accomplishments:

• A long-established mention in Canadian historical records, albeit much of it negative or controversial (Daniels, 1979; Verrall and Keeshig-Tobias, 1987);

• A significant body of literature pertaining to their heritage and culture (Friesen & Lusty, 1980; Verrall and Keeshig-Tobias, 1987; Barkwell, Dorion, and Préfontaine, 2001);

• Formation of distinct communities in western Canada (Gordon, 1964, 70; Friesen, 1985: 113-115; Purich, 1988, 28; Peterson, 2001: 41);

• Recognition of unique community life by provincial governments and museums (Dobbin, 1981; Brasser, 2001: 228);

• Development of a unique cultural pattern including a belief system, social structure, symbolic elements, arts and skills and festivals, for example, the annual buffalo hunt (Sealey and Lussier, 1975, 23; Redbird, 1980; Friesen, 1983, 1-2; Spry, 2001: 97-99);

• Formulation of a governing charter (Charlebois, 1975);

• Political persistence in flying three flags (Friesen & Lusty, 1980);

• Definite cultural contributions to the Canadian way of life including the introduction of European technology to the prairies (Smith, 1985: 58);

• Regarded as unique and different with a separate and distinct identity by incoming Europeans (Smith, 1985: 50; Mailhot and Sprague, 1985);

• The target of negative perceptions and actions by neighboring cultural groups who by their behavior confirmed the reality of the Métis lifestyle. This behavior also served to forge defensive aspects of a Métis identity (Woodcock, 1976; Sprenger, 1978, 118; Friesen, 1984; Friesen, 1996; Dusenberry, 2001: 131); and,

• A continuing positive self-image (Peters, Rosenberg, and Halseth, 1991; Roberts, von Below, and Bos, 2001: 193).

It would be somewhat demeaning to the Métis cause to ignore the impact of the above evidence. The degree to which the basic criteria for cultural uniqueness have been met by the Métis people tends to substantiate their claims and cannot easily be disregarded. Despite this reality, the struggle for recognition as an equal partner in the deliberations regarding Canada's future remains an ongoing challenge for the Métis people.

A Note on Historiography

For the past century it has become quite customary to trace Métis history by describing the "Riel Rebellions" of 1869 and 1885.

Today some writers have softened the negative image of the Métis by down-writing the Riel Wars using other, less contrary forms of language to describe those events, for example, civil wars, resistance movements, cultural conflicts, reactionary struggles or hostilities. As history continues to unfold and public attitudes towards Native peoples change, perhaps using the concept of rebellion when it was really resistance that was being enacted, will disappear completely from the historical writing. If public perceptions of Aboriginal peoples do shift to a more positive stance it will because of the efforts made by the Indigenous peoples to tell their side of the story.

As a further indicator of negativity towards the Métis cause, it used to be common in both governmental documents as well as other literature to use the words, "halfbreeds" or "breeds," to denote the heritage of Native people of mixed blood. Since the time of the publication of the book, *Halfbreed*, by Maria Campbell (1973), however, the word halfbreed has fallen into disrepute and the terms Métis or nonStatus Aboriginal have been substituted. Although its use is not necessarily legally or biologically correct, the word nonStatus Indian can refer to several different categories of Native people, that is, Aboriginals who have lost their Status, those who have Indian bloodlines but never attained legal Status, or members of Métis culture who could but choose not to lay claim to that particular identity.

In addition to the matter of shifts in vocabulary is the manner in which the Métis have been portrayed through the various epochs of Canadian history. For a long time one of the only positive historical treatments of their story was provided by Auguste-Henri de Tremaudan (1982), a French businessman who gained an interest in the Métis when he edited a local newspaper in The Pas, Manitoba, during the first few decades of this century. His book was not completed at the time of his death in 1929, but with the help of some editors from the Union Nationale Métisse, the work was finally published in 1935. The primary difficulty with de Tremaudan's work is the controversy emanating from the book's appendix which he did not write. Critics have accused de Tremaudan of interviewing only biased witnesses pertaining to the happenings after 1885, thereby making the Métis look good and the Roman Catholic Church look bad. To counteract de Tremaudan's untruths, a harsh critic, Father A. G. Morice, travelled to Batoche to do his own interviewing of 1885 survivors. Apparently he found the very opposite of what de Tremaudan was alleged to have discovered, namely that the Roman Catholic Church was without fault in the matter.

Later, another critic, Donatien Fremont, editor of the French language newspaper, *La Liberte,* claimed that the Métis were forced to take up arms in 1885 and encouraged to apostatize the church. He claimed that Riel had overtaken the church at Saint Antoine de Padou and had made the clergy his prisoners. Riel had apparently passed himself off as a priest and heard confessions from his followers. Naturally, the Riel's people demanded and got equal space in Fremont's newspaper, but the debate got so heated that eventually local residents even banned the newspaper from their community. Still, none of this meets the fact that the troublesome passage in de Tremaudan's book is the appendix, which members of the Union Nationale Métisse wrote, not de Tremaudan himself (Lussier, 1982: xxi-xxiv).

Sprague (1988) claims that historians have not always been very objective in reviewing events and happenings related to the Métis. In fact, he claims, these writers have done a better job in reflecting their times than in analyzing historical events. Lower (1977) was probably the historian who most positively assessed the place of the Métis in Canada, but his work is either ignored or overlooked in Sprague's account. Lower suggested that the Métis were clearly dealt out of their lands in Manitoba. In 1946 he pointed out there was evidence for believing that the surveyors whom Riel accosted not only trespassed but also talked boastfully about taking Canada over, implying that the Métis would have their lands confiscated. According to Lower, this was one of the major causes of the "Rebellion" of 1869 (Lower, 1977: 357). George Stanley, whose book, *The Birth of Western Canada,* appeared in 1936, considered the Natives a failure (1960). Their tragedy was to be doomed as a people. He accused the Métis of standing against the march of "civilization," so they were pushed aside to make a way for newcomers. Stanley argued that even the Métis resistance was an absurd act.

Another historian of high standing, W.L. Morton (1957), offered a different reason for the eventual Métis rise and downfall, namely that the Métis were cheated by the failure of major institutions like the federal government and the Hudson's Bay Company to do justice to their communities. Giraud (1956), apparently denounced Métis land claims on the grounds that they had been defeated in battle; and that was that. An even more debilitating case against the Métis was posed by historian Donald Creighton (1955) who depicted Louis Riel as a national nuisance and denounced the claims of the Métis as dubious at best.

More recently, Thomas Flanagan of the University of Calgary has argued that the Métis have no valid claim to being considered "Aboriginal people" since they were not even in existence at the time of first contact and the announcement of the Royal Proclamation of 1763 (Flanagan, 1979a). Negative descriptions of the Métis continue to appear. In describing Louis Riel's return to Canada in 1884 to aid his people, historian Peter Waite (2002: 354) suggests that Riel was taunted "for having accomplished nothing. A Riel put on his mettle was dangerous." Riel apparently lost the support of the Roman Catholic Church because of his claim to be a prophet and his threats of militarism.

By the end of the 1960s most nonNative Canadian historians abandoned interest in the Riel/Métis phenomenon and turned their research efforts elsewhere. Soon thereafter several Métis individuals, having successfully moved into the world of academe, began to write about their own people (Sealey and Kirkness, 1973; Adams, 1975; Sealey and Lussier, 1975; LaRoque, 1975; and Lussier and Sealey, 1978). The result was that books with an entirely different historical perspective began to appear on library shelves. These new writers purported to present the Métis interpretation of events surrounding their fate. Their claims were paralleled by a different, more kindly rendition of the Métis in biographical books about Louis Riel, for example, Bowsfield's fair and exhaustive evaluation (1971), Howard's historical novel (1974), and Charlebois' rather defensive account (1975). In addition, a large number of works by less well-known Native writers appeared who either wrote valuable histories or ably defended their cause (Friesen & Lusty, 1980).

Most analytical works on the Métis in the decade of the 1990s adopted an either-or stance on the subject, that is, those who believed that the Métis were short-changed in the past and those who believed that the Métis were either treated fairly or merely misrepresented their case. At first glance it appears that those who have something to gain by denying Métis claims, have done so. Historians Gerhard Ens (1988) and Thomas Flanagan would appear to fall into this category of writers since they were retained by the Canadian Department of Justice in 1986 to defend Canada from Métis land claims (Sprague, 1991: 138). Mailhot and Sprague (1985), on the other hand, argued on the side of the Métis, although Flanagan (1991a) contends that the Manitoba Métis Federation garnered Sprague's cooperation, for whatever reason, and influenced his stance to incline favorably towards their case. Sprague's perspective is shared by Purich (1988) although it does not appear that the latter's position has any political or financial strings attached.

Writing in *Canadian Geographic* (March/April, 2003: 70-80), Linda Goyette concurs with Purich that the Métis were swindled by the federal government, unscrupulous land spectators, and other groups. Goyette claims that signatures were forged and impersonators posing as Métis stood in line to receive scrip certificates. Goyette relies on research undertaken by the MatriX Project of Edmonton, funded by the Canadian government, the Government of Saskatchewan, and the Métis National Council. MatriX is headed by Frank Tough, Director of the School of Native Studies at the University of Alberta.

Tough's project began as investigation to support a massive Métis land claim in northern Saskatchewan undertaken in March 1994 by residents of 19 Métis communities. The claim intimates that the Métis of Treaty 10 region in northern Saskatchewan are a distinct people who still occupy lands that have never legally been ceded to them.

Tough and his associates argue that the campaign to cheat the Métis out of their lands involved a number of different parties, possibly also the Roman Catholic Church. Oblate Bishops Pascal and Benard, for example, had 94 claims delivered to them but it is not certain whether the certificates were held in trust for Métis holders or whether the benefits thereof went into church coffers. So far the Oblates have not opened their files to Tough's researchers.

One Lethbridge realtor, Frank Mason, collected Métis scrip for 19 234 acres of land in northwestern Saskatchewan and Alberta. A young Winnipeg student, W. P. Fillmore, described his experiences as scrip collector this way; "I was supposed to act as an independent buyer . . . and was given $5 000 in a canvas bag which I carried in my hip pocket." Many buyers like Fillmore cooperated with each other in order to eliminate competition.

Analysts who disagree with Goyette's stance point out that at the same time as the Métis were laying claim to lands, homesteaders had to pay up to ten dollars for a quarter section of land. A scrip certificate worth 240 dollars could by comparison be deemed an enormous sum. A crucial question that arises in this context is; "Since these claims can apparently so easily be documented and if there was so much skulduggery going on, why did the federal government keep such extensive records?" It also helps to remember that while the Métis were badly done by in terms of government promises, so were many other groups of immigrants such as Chinese, Doukhobors, Japanese, Scandinavians, and Ukrainians.

In a volume of limited size, such as this, it becomes necessary to be careful in selecting subject matter. As a result, this book does not purport to examine the issue of Métis land claims, nor to analyze whether or not the Métis people have been swindled, cheated, or deprived of any rights of citizenship as Aboriginal people. Rather, the intent is that having examined the Métis case for nationhood and cultural distinctiveness, it becomes clear that Canadians need to change their perceptions of this unique community. An examination of historical documentation and Métis culture and lifestyle seem to indicate that the Métis case has definite merit. The conclusion can only be that in light of the ever widening milieu of Canada's multiculturalism, which inherently or at least legally guarantees equal rights to all peoples in the nation, it would be difficult to come to any other conclusion.

2

Identity

Our young men will marry your daughters, and we shall be one people. – Samuel de Champlain, "Father of New France," is supposed to have said on two occasions. (Dickason, 2001: 21)

A Métis was not a French-Canadian, nor a Canadian, nor a Scot. Neither were they First Nations or Inuit. They created for themselves and future generations a unique culture, a group identity and declared themselves a "New Nation." (Lawrence Barkwell and Ed Swain 2001: 1)

As history unfolds and its interpreters unveil the influences by which their opinions have been shaped, newer time-adjusted definitions emerge. This has been the case with the Métis people who today have a better grasp of the outline of their contemporary place in society, but the delineation of that identity has shifted with the times. On some fronts it is still difficult to pinpoint the definition of the word "Métis." The term Métis can refer to individuals and communities who derive some of their cultural practices from nonNative communities whose origins lie in the pre-1870 west. It can also refer to individuals whose circumstances of birth suggest a Métis identity as preferable to the pejorative term halfbreed. At times even nonStatus Indians are referred to as Métis (Foster, 1983: 78). When noted Canadian Métis folksinger Buffy St. Marie was asked if she thought it was appropriate for people to call her a half-breed she deferred saying that she thought she would better be described as a "doublebreed," and she claimed having the best of the two races in her bloodline (Alberta Federation of Métis Settlements, 1978: 13). It is this kind of sharp and insightful response, backed by passionate pride, that has earmarked and maintained a special place for the Métis in the annals of Canadian history.

Perhaps the best definition of Métis is someone who lives according to the Métis lifestyle, considers himself/herself part of that community, and is considered part of the community by their peers. This would appear to coincide with the interpretation of the Supreme Court of Canada. Like the American statement of law, "Everyone must be considered innocent until proven guilty," so are the Métis. They have a right to that identity until their community deems otherwise. Coincidentally, an appropriate answer to the question, "When is a Métis no longer a Métis?" should be: "When he/she no longer considers himself/herself Métis" (Lussier and Sealey, 1978: 188). This position injects a philosophical element into the question of cultural identity and to the interpretation of history, for that matter. As an ancient Greek philosopher named Dionysius of Halicarnassus, stated around 40 B.C., "History is philosophy drawn from examples" (Cohen and Cohen, 1985: 140). If one has an attraction to becoming philosophical about the history or identity of the various segments within the Canadian Native milieu, the Métis provide an intriguing example. Their identity is definitely emerging.

Exploring the Options

Métis origins and history are complex and varied though historians have tended to use the Red River, Manitoba, experience as a guideline by which to elaborate their further impact on the nation. According to the Alberta Federation of Métis Settlement Association (1978), in a book designed for Alberta schools, it all started in 1816 (with the Battle of Seven Oaks), because at that time a new nation of people was born in Canada. Métis roots may be much older than that, however; some historians have jokingly pointed out that the Métis had their origin nine months after the first Europeans landed in the Americas. Purich (1988: 15) notes that there may be some truth to the joke for people of mixed blood were noted in the annals of Canadian history in Nova Scotia in the early 1600s.

The word "Métis" is derived from the French and simply means people of mixed blood. When the fur traders and other Europeans came to Canada, many of them intermarried with Aboriginals, and the children of these marital unions obviously had mixed blood. Although there were possibly as many as 14 different European peoples living in Western Canada in the final decades of the nineteenth century, it is the French, Crees, and Ojibway who are credited with giving birth to the Métis. That said, it is still a complex matter to determine who can lay claim to being Métis today. Certainly the argument for bloodlines is spurious since each succeeding generation will obviously be attached by a weaker link.

In an attempt to lend specificity to the topic, it may be helpful to outline the various ways in which the Métis people have been defined in Canada. A generic definition implies that all Native peoples who are not registered as Status Indians via the Indian Act may be called Métis. It is estimated that there are at least a million such Canadians, but many of them certainly do not think of themselves as being Métis, and they do not live a lifestyle which in any way represents Métis philosophy, beliefs or values.

The difficulty of differentiating the identities of Native peoples on the basis of the Indian Act raises the intriguing question of ancestry and Indian Status. Since Status was originally assigned on a happenstance basis, that is, those First Nations who stood in line to be registered obtained Status. Their bloodlines or cultural affiliations were not investigated and as a result, many individuals with some degree of nonNative ancestry also legally became Indians. Many people in Canada may exhibit all the social, cultural, and racial attributes of "Indianness," but they are not defined as Indians in the legal sense (Frideres and Gadacz, 2001: 24f). By way of example, there are groups of full-blooded Indians in Newfoundland who are not legally considered Indians because at the time when Newfoundland joined Canada, both Ottawa and the Newfoundland government ignored the issue (Purich, 1988: 9). The situation in Labrador is quite unique in that the resident Métis are the country's only "Inuit Métis." Although many Labrador Métis have Innu and to a lesser extent Micmac heritage, more than 80 percent are Inuit descendants (Hanrahan, 2000: 234).

In the western regions of Canada there are accounts that members of Indian bands were out hunting when the enumeration process was underway in their community and thus their names never made it into the government register. This leads to the conclusion that while Aboriginal leaders today are fighting to preserve their traditional cultural heritage, it is not an ancestry without biological implications. In addition, the vicissitudes of history have decreed that many full-blooded First Nations, through accident, will be deterred from making their cultural contribution because they have been written out of the Canadian First Nations record.

In recent years a variety of Indian and Métis organizations have sprung up to argue a stronger case for Aboriginal rights. Many of their efforts have centred on the struggle to regain lost rights either through accident, omission, or legal changes. Some interpreters have chosen to concentrate on specific historical happenings as a basis for determining such identity. These claims are supported by evidence that a specific Métis culture developed in the Red River area in the early 1800s during the reign of the Hudson's Bay Company. The content of that culture included worldview, patterns of clothing, food, and folkways, but more than that it also featured a participation mystique, or a desire of the people to come together (Redbird, 1980). Against these observations the Métis National Council has defined Métis identity as including all individuals who can show they are descendants of persons considered Métis under the 1870 Manitoba Act, the Dominion Lands Acts of 1879 and 1883, or by proving through other means that they have been accepted as Métis by the Métis community (Purich, 1988: 13).

Perhaps the most reliable route to determining Métis identity originates within the Métis community itself. As time continues to delineate distinctions among members of First Nations, the Métis have expressed a wish to outline their own conditions of membership. This is a departure from past decades when Native leaders generically preferred to think of themselves as "separate from the white mainstream world" (Adams, 1975: x). In many regions the Métis were once considered a vital part of the total Aboriginal community, and there was no independent Métis society apart from those operating on behalf of Indigenous peoples generally.

In a study of its membership conducted by the Ontario Métis and Non-Status Association in 1985 it was found that a strong sense of identity was based on Aboriginal ancestry, but without reliance on any specific Native language. Additional valued entities in the gleaned list included preference for a legal status, (apart from that of other Native peoples), a desire for a distinct land base, political representation and separate institutions dedicated to preserving Native culture (Peters, Rosenberg and Halseth, 1991). These criteria tend to emphasize the specifics of a formalized delineation of Métis identity, rather than affirming Redbird's concept of a people's "mystique." Today, individuals in many Aboriginal communities are in the painful process of developing their identity, and while the outcome will, hopefully, result in clearly identifiable characteristics, these will no doubt be spawned out of insights gleaned from very deep emotions and feelings (LaRoque, 1975: 14).

The Quest for Identity

A number of Métis writers have outlined the options available to their people in seeking to further their continuing quest to impact Canadian society. Even here a transition of conceptualization is evident, and a more political perspective is emerging. A generation ago, University of Saskatchewan Professor Howard Adams decried the faults of the capitalistic system which served only to suppress Native people. He observed that, "The ballot box is clearly not the way we are going to achieve liberation" (Adams, 1975: 201). Adams maintained that for a limited percentage of the Métis population, liberation would come only through integration with the dominant WASP society. This would require that individuals would learn how the various political institutions of dominant society operate, and infiltrate them and absorb the inherent lifestyle. The preferred route for this undertaking would be schooling (Friesen & Lusty, 1980: vii). For the masses of Native people, however, fate would assign them to a ghetto. Adams insisted that the way out would be to overthrow the institutions of imperialism and colonization, by violent means if necessary. He believed that this concept would attract Métis followers and snowball into a national Native movement. Support from the people would come as soon as they saw the possibility of improvement in their conditions and developed a desire to change the system. To date Adams' plan has not been acted upon. Instead Métis leaders have resorted to education, politics, and the courts.

During the 1970s Adams' thinking was parallelled to a degree by Bruce Sealey and Antoine Lussier of the Manitoba Métis Federation. These writers deplored the living conditions of Native communities, Métis particularly, but they realized that the majority of the Métis people rarely even considered the possibility of national segregation. Their solution was that governments should develop mechanisms by which to react quickly and effectively to the social and economic needs of the Métis. Failure to do so would induce a significant Canadian cultural group to turn from seeking improvement through peaceful means to more desperate measures. Unlike the more militant Adams, who was quick to sketch out at least the parameters of planned revolution, Sealey and Lussier pulled back to suggest that "the deplorable social and economic conditions existing will, unless corrected, lead inevitably to racial violence in many parts of Canada" (Sealey, and Lussier, 1975: 194).

The radicalism of Howard Adams was not universally endorsed by the Métis of Canada, and many leaders offered a more subdued approach. David Courchene (1973), for example, suggested that the resolve to alleviate the lamentable living conditions of the Native peoples would have to come from within their community. He concurred that the national financial cost would be tremendous, but it would have to be borne by the nation in order to minimize conflict and frustration for future generations. Courchene believed in the "love and goodwill" approach to socioeconomic improvement, and endorsed such phrases as "learning to understand one another, living in accordance with the precepts of the brotherhood of man, and the need for mutual understanding and mutual support" (Courchene, 1973: 181-182). His position was shared by the majority of his colleagues who pled for empathy and understanding instead of criticism and judgement (Kirkness, 1973; LaRoque, 1975). A more reluctant contemporary, Marie Campbell, concurred by offering these words, "I realize that an armed revolution of Native people will never come about; even if such a thing were possible, what would it accomplish?" (Campbell, 1973: 156).

Today's generation of Métis have adopted a philosophical middle ground between revolution and love and kindness; they have begun to familiarize themselves with the legal sector. This stance logistically implies a more exacting and legally couched definition of Métis people and, as earlier indicated, is a delineation tied not only to history but also to a land base (Peters, Rosenberg and Halseth, 1991). This approach has paid off, as the supreme court decision of September 19, 2003 has shown.

The Métis quest for a land base had a good starting point in 1966 when the Saskatchewan Métis took the provincial Liberal government to court over land rights in Green Lake. Although the government lost the battle, they responded by launching a vicious campaign of intimidation and bribery in the Green Lake community. Local civil servants were told their jobs were on the line unless they worked to get rid of the radical element in the community. Métis leaders Jim Brady and Malcolm Norris, were targeted for negative press by government in an effort to dissuade them from influencing the community and stirring their people to political action (Dobbin, 1981: 224f). Still, the event bore fruit and was duplicated by similar developments in several other provinces. By the early 1970s the federal government made a marked departure from their traditional approach and widened its historic dealings with Native peoples to include Métis and nonStatus Indians. Within the decade the government also began to address Métis and nonStatus issues even though the government perspective and that of the two groups were frequently at variance. By the mid-1970s special programs for Aboriginal people, using the wider, generic sense of the term, had been developed by at least seven governmental departments and agencies. Possibly the most significant of these programs was the "core funding policy" through which Native political organizations at both the provincial and federal levels could continue to put pressure on a host of federal departments, thus keeping Aboriginal issues before ministers and senior officials (Weaver, 1985: 80-102).

In the early 1980s the Métis people put together a national consultative group as a forum to share ideas about cross-country issues. Simultaneously, there have been ongoing constitutional reform talks, plans for Native socioeconomic development and the origination of new programs through the Western Development Fund. It was difficult for the consultative group to get a handle on all of these activities and still serve as a policy formulation body at the same time. By 1982 the group had disbanded, but not before they convinced the federal government explicitly to recognize the Métis as one of Canada's Aboriginal peoples in the Constitution. The counterpart to this major symbolic victory came shortly thereafter when the government denied the legal validity of the Native Council of Canada's land claims submission but confirmed its continuing concern for Métis and nonStatus Indians' socio-economic conditions. These communities could only interpret these developments as a government-created political reality whose existence denies, but whose presence frustrates constructive persons and ideas inside and outside government (Weaver, 1985: 97-98).

As the formalization of Métis and nonStatus Indian identity continues to develop, one cannot but be struck by the reality that finances are a big factor in determining the direction and impact of the deliberation process. Purich (1988) suggests that improvement can come in three ways: first, economic development schemes could be established which would give rise to a tax base. This would require additional federal capital. Second, governments could surrender control of some resource income to Métis communities, for example, the ownership of minerals. This would provide an income to those communities. Third, is the matter of equalization money which could be transferred to Native governments in the same way as monies are made available to have-not provinces (Purich, 1988: 201). Naturally, this process implies a great deal of interchange and consultation with the Métis communities, but these proposals appear to be a realistic starting point.

Against the Odds

The path pursued by Métis leaders to obtain an adequate land base by which to undergird their claims to a long Canadian heritage is not without its roadblocks. Although the bulk of analysts have probably come down on the side of the Métis in acknowledging their having been unfairly treated in the past, their opponents have been equally vociferous in denouncing Métis claims. In 1978, the Manitoba Métis Federation claimed that after the Red River experience Métis lands had been bought and sold through fraud, forgery, and speculation (Manitoba Métis Federation, 1978). This position has been supported by Purich who observes that "There can be no question that outright fraud was committed against some Métis. All that remains unknown is the extent of the fraud" (Purich, 1988: 125).

A decade ago the Manitoba Métis Federation enlisted the help of University of Manitoba historian, D.N. Sprague, to document the background to Métis land claims. Sprague discovered the

Canadian government, under the leadership of Prime Minister John A. Macdonald, actually tried to rid the Province of Manitoba of the Métis population in order to make room for more European settlers. Sprague argues that Macdonald deliberately provoked the Saskatchewan Métis into joining Riel's campaign to ensure that Parliament would vote funds for the Canadian Pacific Railway. Sprague's thesis is supported by another Manitoba writer, Gerhard Ens, who argues that the Government of Manitoba encouraged the sale of Métis children's allotments and the effort was supported by politicians, lawyers, and judges alike (Ens, 1983). Canadian historian, Gerald Friesen (1984), concurs with this diagnosis, and observes that either the politicians involved in the activity were dishonest or they simply permitted speculators to attain unwarranted monetary gains. In any event, the Métis were cheated.

Almost a lone voice sounding out the opinion of the opposition, Thomas Flanagan of The University of Calgary, decries the work of Sprague, Ens, and Friesen and laments that the notion that the Métis were cheated is ". . . finding its way into the general literature of Canadian history . . ." (Flanagan, 1991a: 7). Flanagan believes that Sprague lacked evidence to support his thesis, Ens' work pertained to only a small percentage of Métis people (less than ten percent), and Friesen was merely quoting Ens (Flanagan, 1991a: 6-8). In addition, a Native writer, Irene Spry made a convincing plea on behalf of the Métis, but according to Flanagan relied too heavily ". . . on an old man's uncorroborated memory" in supporting her argument (Flanagan, 1991a: 9).

At the root of the argument about Métis land claims is the Manitoba Act of 1870 which was entrenched in the constitution by the first amendment of the British North America Act in 1871. Section 31 of the Act states that:

> . . . the Lieutenant-Governor shall select such lots or tracts in such parts of the Province [of Manitoba] as he shall deem expedient, to the extent aforesaid and divide the same among the children of the half-breed of families residing in the Province at the time of said transfer to Canada, and the same shall be granted to the said children respectively in such mode and on such conditions as to settlement and otherwise, as the Governor-General in Council may from time to time determine. (Flanagan, 1991a: 112)

It is Flanagan's position that the federal government generally fulfilled, and in some ways overfulfilled, the land provisions of the Manitoba Act. Naturally, Métis leaders disagree, and the result has been a series of court cases. The Métis won the first round in 1987, but the decision was overturned the following year by the Manitoba Appeal Court. Since then legal arguments and court cases have continued, all of which makes the September 19, 2003, decision of the Supreme Court of Canada so important. The Métis face a multi-faceted challenge combining claims and questions about an identity grounded in legalities and ground space. In the meantime, the Alberta Métis Nation, for example, has forged ahead on its conviction that a healthy land base is a definite source of power. To that end Métis leaders have been investing in real estate in Calgary and Edmonton to the extent that ". . . they are now a major landlord in Alberta's two biggest cities" (*Alberta Report*, January 13, 1992). Add to this reality the prognosis of Native writer, Joseph Couture, about the perseverance of Native people and the future looks a good deal brighter for the Métis. Couture (1985: 6-7) contends that the contemporary challenge to maintain cultural identity will only serve to bring out the best in the Native community; after all, the Native community includes responses to challenges within the dominant Canadian society that reveal a greater diversity than any other Canadian group. Aboriginal cultures are dynamic, adaptive and adapting, not limited to the past. Improved education and familiarity with mainstream institutional practices has motivated the new generation of Métis to demand recognition of their special status as Canadians. As Thomas (2001: 246) notes,

> . . . there is a striving on the part of some educated Métis for the legitimization of the Métis as a people by the outside society, either as a 'native' people or as a group apart with a unique history and national consciousness.

3
Ingenuity

The Métis were unique among native people in the sense that as distinct entities they did not antedate the fur trade. They alone could look to the fur trade for their origins and not simply for significant influences. (John E. Foster, *The New Peoples*, 2001: 73)

In fact the Métis are pioneers of multiculturalism. One has only to read the history of Western Canada to recognize the contributions of the Métis to the national ethic. Harry W. Daniels, *We Are the New Nation*, 1979: 51)

Longevity of being and uniqueness of origin are usually cited as significant characteristics of ethnocultural identity, and the Métis are no exception in making their case. Apparently the longevity of a culture lends validity to its existence and provides a kind of assurance for the future stability for cultural adherents. A decade or two ago, when the "roots" syndrome hit North America, partially motivated by the movie of that name, it sent many subcultural groups scurrying in search of their origins. Partially fuelled by the enunciation of Canada's multicultural policy, with its addendum of minimal funding for being ethnic (Friesen, 1992: 25), it is quite likely that the search for roots syndrome will continue well into the twenty-first century.

In the case of the Métis, their history incorporates more than a century of the Canadian past accompanied by claims to a specific land space once governed under three separate flags developed in 1816, 1869, and 1880. At the time of Confederation the Métis comprised a unique cultural entity and they were a military might to be reckoned with (McLean, 1988: 47). The Métis became a unique part of northern Canadian history from the time of the beginning of the fur trade partly because of their exclusion from other cultural groups in Canada. Many families moved westward from Rupert's

Land where they had originated and relocated to the west in quest of land, or fur or simply to seek adventure with the Hudson's Bay Company. By the late 1890s a number of Métis had settled in the Athabasca-Mackenzie District, and the NWMP Commissioner in Regina Laurence William Herchmer, expressed fear that the Métis could influence treaty negotiations with the Indians. As an indication of the extent of influence which the Métis held in the nation at that time, Herchmer suggested that the federal government negotiate with the Métis as well as the Indians in settling land claims (Fumoleau, 1973: 58). The status of the Métis, in his estimation, was significant enough that they should be regarded as a separate legal and cultural entity in land negotiations.

The Métis today can forge a strong argument that their place in Canadian history is unique and cannot be glossed over. Their origin in the era of the fur trade attests to this, and historical documentation pertaining thereto is growing, much of it authored by Métis writers (Friesen & Lusty, 1980; Verrall and Keeshig-Tobias, 1987; Barkwell, Dorion, and Préfontaine, 2001; Peterson and Brown, 2001). Government records and documents remain a primary source, but analytic writings by Native and nonNative writers are increasing. The works produced by Métis writers and organizations tend to be apologetic, both lamenting the lack of past regard as well as making the case for a unified Métis front.

No one could envisage the impact that European ways would have on Aboriginal culture, and initially the resultant arrangement comprised an advantageous tradeoff for both sides. Cree First Nations, for example, liked the trade goods which the incoming Europeans made available, and they were eager to provide an ample supply of furs to appease European appetites (Friesen, 1991a: 7). As the fur trade pushed further west some Aboriginal First Nations, like Crees and Ojibways, followed the trade and eventually relocated both their hunting territories and their winter grounds. By the mid-seventeenth century a cultural separation developed between the Woodland Crees and the Plains Crees that has remained to this day, and has resulted in fairly significant distinctions in lifestyle.

Fur Trading Companies

On May 2nd, 1970, King Charles II granted to the Governor and the Company of Adventurers of England Trading into Hudson's Bay the sole trade and commerce of all the seas, straits, bays, rivers, lakes and sounds in the Hudson's Bay Territory and surrounding areas then known as Rupert's Land. The total land space included about a third of a million acres (Howard, 1974). Estimates are that the ceded area included the geographic living areas of about 50 000 Aboriginal peoples basically made up of three linguistic groups, Algonkians, Athapaskans, and Sioux. Further subdivisions revealed these distinctions: Algonkians, which included the Cree, Ojibway, Saulteaux, and the three member nations of the Blackfoot Confederacy – Blackfoot (now called Siksika), Peigan (Pikiunis), and Blood (Kainai); Athapaskans, which included the Sarcees (Tsuu T'ina), the Beavers (from whom the Tsuu T'ina originated), Chipewyans, and other northern tribes; and the Sioux represented by the Stoney or Assiniboine Indians, and a few wandering Sioux from the United States (Stanley, 1960).

Early historical descriptions of the first Aboriginal and European contacts were furnished by explorers and fur traders. Henry Kelsey set out to identify the Indigenous tribes of the interior in 1690, Arthur Henday spent the winter with the Blackfoot tribe in 1754, and Matthew Cocking replicated Henday's trip in 1772. Each, in turn, provided information about an important period of Canadian history. From the beginning, the exploitation of the fur trade constituted a mutual goal for both the English and the French, and while the English were laying claim to Rupert's Land from Hudson Bay, the French were pushing up the St. Lawrence Valley. By the year 1800s a full-fledged rivalry was underway between two fur trading companies, the North West Company and the Hudson's Bay Company.

The North West Company was founded in the late 1770s by an alliance of French and Scottish interests following the defeat of the French on the Plains of Abraham in 1759. The Hudson's Bay Company, on the other hand, originated a century earlier, in 1670, of English interests (Lower, 1977). Ironically, two disillusioned Frenchmen assisted in its formation, Pierre-Esprit Radisson and Medard Chouart Des Groseilliers (Mr. Radish and Mr. Gooseberry, as the English translated their names), who directed the English to the rich fur trading areas south of Hudson and James Bay. Finding no support in New France for their plan of trading in the area, the two went over to the English (Francis, Jones, and Smith, 1988: 104).

By 1800s it is estimated that the two fur trading rival companies permanently employed from 1 500 to 2 000 men in the Northwest, and since the number of women was small, the traders often formed liaisons with Native women. The officials of the Hudson's Bay Company looked with disdain on these unions although they recognized their "commercial value" in terms of furthering better relations with the Indians for trading purposes. As the next century developed, it was observed that there were very few employees of the company who did not contact alliances with Aboriginal women in the neighborhoods of the trading posts. Allegedly, many of these liaisons were temporary, and when a company employee terminated a particular assignment and returned to "civilization," he was expected to abandon his children and their mother. In no situations was the father allowed to take his mixed-blood children back to Europe. As a result, his Native partner either formed a new relationship or returned to her cultural habitat (Stanley, 1960: 6). The relationships that endured revealed a considerable effort on the part of Native females to adjust to "civilization," and often the attachments between members of such intercultural connections revealed both a caring sensitivity and a strong personal commitment.

As time passed it became evident that the greater number of intercultural unions were formed between French (particularly those connected to the North West Trading Company), and First Nations (Cree and Ojibway) people. It was this racial and cultural combination that formed the roots of the Métis culture as it developed, even though the term today is not without its complications and denotes almost any kind of mix of nonNative with Indian ancestry. Native-nonNative liaisons were officially discouraged in eighteenth century New France and this regulation aided in fostering a separate identity for the Métis. Eventually, separate Métis communities formed, featuring distinct identities and often attracting adherents who preferred the freedom and opportunities of life in Aboriginal country to the regulations of church and state in established settlements. Their mixed-blood offspring formed the nuclei of new settlements at several dozen different localities in eastern Canada (Brown, 1987).

Métis Settlements

An outstanding characteristic of the emerging Métis identity was the formation of distinct communities, quite different in nature from those of either their European or Aboriginal parental origins. The first Métis settlements were built at Fort William (now Thunder Bay, Ontario), and at the juncture of the Red and Assiniboine Rivers (now Winnipeg, Manitoba). Other settlements included Pembina, Hair Hills, and Deer Lake in the Manitoba area, and Fort des Prairies (now Edmonton) and in other Alberta locations such as Lac La Biche, Lac Ste. Anne, and Lesser Slave Lake (Purich, 1988: 28). In many ways the lifestyle of these settlements resembled that of their nonNative affiliations, but the Métis also developed unique distinctives. Métis men, for example, wore what became a familiar insignia of their culture, a blue capote (cloak), a red belt, and corduroy trousers. The belt was a simple badge of distinction and though the Europeans wore it over their cloaks, the Métis wore it under theirs.

The Métis manner of earning a living included farming and home construction, and fur trade-related occupations in which role they acted as interpreters, intermediaries, and distributors. The Métis also attended Roman Catholic religious worship services and developed courts of justice much like their French paternal ancestors. The church figured prominently in settlement life where marriage unions were blessed and baptisms were performed. During the seventeenth century, French officials supported interracial marriages in hopes of furthering their policy of "frenchification" which consisted of converting Indigenous peoples and attempting to build up the population of the new country. By the eighteenth century the policy shifted somewhat against intermarriage, partly because of an increase in the population of nonNative women who were available for marriage. Many European women were specifically imported to marry bachelor settlers (Chalmers, 1974: 11-12). In addition, French nationalists began to worry about their colleagues taking up the "savage" way of life, thus weakening the essence of French culture in the colony (Brown, 1987: 137). During this time the mixed Native population of the emerging nation was never separately identified in the official record other than as an informal notation of "the natives of Hudson's Bay" (Brown, 1987: 139). Historians like Giraud were harsh in their criticisms of Métis national potential. Giraud (1986: 479) observed that

> . . . there existed, neither in their material culture, not in their personality, nor in their achievements, any element that was really likely to provide a foundation for their national ideal.

The Métis were perceived as neither Aboriginal nor European, and thus, individually or in groups, sided with whichever cultural community would accept them. Bourgeault (1983: 79) suggests that the Métis came into being as a result of the internal formation of a "class" structure within the mercantile capitalism of the fur trade. The nature of the struggle plagued Métis workers from two sides. On the one side, they had to work for the North West Company, and they had to buy goods from the company. On the other side was the fact that those who worked for Métis businessmen instead of the North West Company fared no better. Métis businessmen paid them just as poorly as the company did (Dobbin, nd: 2).

It might be noted that with the exception of the Manitoba experience, the Métis probably lacked the distinct community and economic base upon which to build a separate identity. However, the Manitoba base was sufficient to fan a spark into a fullblown flame. As Morton (1939: 130) put it, "Nationalism born of racial feelings and nurtured by a common language and by a community of interests is an undying flame." The Métis thirst for recognition and self-consciousness was clearly a Manitoba phenomenon, but it has proven to be a catalyst to spirit the patriotism of their membership into the twenty-first century.

Red River Colony Life

Although there is no official record about the precise beginnings of the Métis Red River settlement, by the outset of the nineteenth century it was a flourishing community. In time a kind of unity developed among the residents including those of both Métis (French and Cree) extraction and those of halfbreed (largely Scottish and Aboriginal) background. The group was cut off from much of European expansion by the accident of geography and thus developed a strong spirit of independence. They were very proud of the elements of their unique cultural identity and accomplishments and they did not consider themselves attached to mainstream white society. Spry (2001: 97) argues that there is insufficient evidence to indicate that the halfbreed and Métis did not get along. In fact their bond of unity was fostered by their ties of blood and long associations in hunting and trading.

The development of several distinct elements unique to Métis culture support their case for historic authenticity. First and foremost was the emergence of the Michif language which is a mixture of Algonquian Cree and French with a few contributions from the Saulteaux language. Essentially the language uses French for nouns and Cree for verbs, thereby comprising two different sets of grammatical rules. Although not classified as a separate language because of its syncretic nature, Michif nicely represents the mixed nature of Métis culture. Essentially a domestic language, Michif is unique to itself in terms of its make-up and cannot be defined as belonging to a single language family (Bakker, 2001: 177). Métis culture and the Michif language are uniquely representative of one another.

Second, no culture would be complete without its artistic forms of expression and the Métis are no exception. Their highly decorated skin coats, pouches, moccasins, and horse gear were visual expressions of this fact, supplemented by their unique form of music and art. Using floral designs, Métis women created a style marked by both complexity and "sparkling delicacy" (Racette, 2001: 182). Clothing is sometimes described as a means of signifying affiliation, and in the case of the Métis, that expression was obvious. Other forms of artistic bent were evident also in the construction of material artifacts, crafts, and tools. Emphasis on Canadian multiculturalism by the federal government in the 1960s brought to life a variety of Métis art forms such as painting, literature, and beadwork embroidery, and as a result the work of a number of Métis artists sprang to national attention (Mattes, 2001: 190). Anyone even remotely acquainted with Métis history is familiar with the highly acclaimed Métis fiddle music and the Red River Jig.

Like their cultural make-up, Métis music and dance are a synthesis of Scottish, Irish, French, and Aboriginal origins, mainly passed on via the oral tradition (Whidden, 2001: 172). McLean (1987: 45) suggests that the Red River jig is based on a pattern of rhythm borrowed a thousand years ago by Plains Indians from the incredible mating dance of the male prairie chicken. Once seen, it is not easily forgotten. The Red River jig is not a highly structured dance, although it does have a basic pattern, and allows for individual variations of the dance steps. In addition to serving as a cultural practice of the past, it is often the basis of individual dance competitions sponsored by various Métis organizations.

Louis Riel was himself a poet and songwriter, and his talents are supplemented by a variety of Métis artists today. Like other subcultures in multicultural Canada, the Métis have a right to expect government support for their kind of cultural pursuit (Roberts, von Below, and Bos, 2001: 197). Riel, by the way, never published any of his poetry although his poems are said to take up about 500 manuscript pages. Riel's poetry contains political and religious content as well as including folksongs, fables, and love poems. One of his poems entitled, Incendium, composed entirely in Latin, is autobiographical (Campbell, 1983: 96).

A third factor in producing a community pride on behalf of the Western Canadian Métis was the negative way their lifestyle was viewed and described by their immigrant Anglo-Saxon counterparts. The latter noted that the Métis' love of open spaces and for the freedom of hunting prevented them from becoming "sensible and steady farmers." Basically, it was said that the Métis despised agriculture and preferred to substitute participation in the annual buffalo hunt to becoming typical participants in the vicissitudes of imported European lifestyle. Thus it was that eminent historians, missionaries, and explorers described them in their writings as "indolent, thoughtless, improvident, unrestrained in their desires, restless, clannish, vain, and irresponsible" (Sprenger, 1978: 118). Against that kind of prosaic portrayal the only logical recourse for the Métis would be to formulate a cultural antidote in the form of a strong sense of peoplehood.

Annual Buffalo Hunt

One of the highlights of Red River life was the annual buffalo hunt which provided the community with the bulk of its subsistence. With a plentiful bounty of food and hides laid up for the winter season, the men could take plenty of time for leisure, including storytelling, music, philosophy, and the development of the arts (Sealey and Lussier, 1975: 23).

In an unpublished essay written by Victoria Callihoo (1945) at the age of 87, she describes aspects of the annual Alberta hunt in this way.

> I was thirteen years old when I first joined in a buffalo hunt. . . . Our main transportation, the Red River cart would be over-hauled. These vehicles did not have any metal in their construc-tion. Large wooden pegs were used where bolts would be used now. Small pegs answered for nails or screws. Cart harness (sic) were made of hides from the buffalo. . . .we usually took three carts along. We had no axle grease and [cooking] grease or tallow was used instead to lubricate the wooden axles. The carts were very squeaky and they could be heard a long way off. Usually there were about one hundred families going on a hunt. . . . We used to cross [the North Saskatchewan] river about where the High Level Bridge [in Edmonton] is now....When the herd was startled, it was just a dark solid moving mass.

A typical Manitoba buffalo hunt could be described as follows. The 1840 hunt, for example, covered 250 miles (400 kilometres) in 19 days. Then the bounty, consisting of over a million pounds (455 000 kilograms) of meat, had to be transported back to the Red River area. Fortuitously, the cunning Métis had developed the famous Red River cart, which proved inextricably handy for this purpose. Basically a two-wheeled wooden form of transport held together by wooden pegs, and pulled by one or two horses or oxen, the cart was light and manoeuvrable and proved to be the key to commercialization. The wheels of the cart were high for conven-ience in traversing rough terrain and the device allowed large quantities of pemmican to be transported hundreds of miles across the prairies; for example, a single cart could carry up to one thou-sand pounds (455 kilograms) of meat (Pelletier, 1977). It also assist-ed the Métis in becoming a semi-settled people instead of persist-ing in their traditional nomadic lifestyle (Sealey and Lussier, 1975: 22).

Traditionally, buffalo were hunted in four major ways on the Canadian prairies. Northern tribes employed the first approach, known as the pound method. In this type of hunt buffalo were chased into a form of terrain specifically containing a naturally-formed blockage that would entrap the animals so they could be killed at will. If the terrain did not easily lend itself to this procedure some tribes would form a human surround and numbers of hunters would stand in formation to force the buffalo to run towards a particular end. This system was quite effective, but very dangerous, particularly if a frantic animal searched out and found a weak point in the line. Often the purpose of the formation was to drive the buffalo into natural traps, such as a bog, where they were likely to flounder and thus present an easy target for the kill. With this method the buffalo were guided into sloughs or blind canyons in the summertime, and in winter they were maneuvered into deep snow drifts or onto thin ice (McHugh, 1972: 62).

The more southerly First Nations tribes often used a second approach known as the buffalo jump method. It involved chasing the buffalo over an embankment so the animals would fall to their death at the bottom of these cliffs. Once the lead animals reached the edge of the precipice it was too late to turn back and they were dashed to their death from the pressure of the oncoming buffalo behind them. By the time the animals landed at the bottom of the cliff many were already dead or disabled. Those that were still alive had their throats cut by hunters waiting at the bottom of the buffalo jump for that purpose. This method was not always negotiated without some degree of challenge in situations when the buffalo were familiar with the terrain. In such instances the hunters would attempt to chase the animals toward an unfamiliar area many kilometres away. It was highly unlikely that the buffalo would have allowed themselves to be chased toward a precipice they knew, no matter how well-concealed the drop-off (McHugh, 1972: 72). One of the best-known buffalo jumps exists in southern Alberta near Fort MacLeod, known as Head-Smashed-In Buffalo Jump.

Preparations for using a buffalo jump were usually quite elaborate. Initially a herd was spotted by herd watchers who informed chiefs and medicine men of the proximity of the herd. The medicine men would say prayers and engage in appropriate rituals, giving thanks for the procuration of food and for the safety for the hunters. The reality was that at times the beasts were as many as 50 to 80 kilometres from the desired jump and they would have to be lured into place. The bison would not naturally line up at a buffalo jump. Luring the animals was done by skilled hunters wearing buffalo robes and mimicking buffalo habits. A long "v" shaped funnel of piles of wood and stones would be erected, often reaching several kilometres away from the jump. If stones and tree branches were scarce on the prairie, hunters would use dried buffalo chips to construct the funnel. It should be noted that buffalo are not blessed with the best of vision, and once the herd got started on a run, the animals tried to avoid any obstacle along the way, rushing pell-mell towards the edge of the cliff. Once inside the funnel, hunters startled the animals into a run towards the embankment at the narrow end of the funnel. A group of older men and hunters waited at the bottom of the embankment to slay any surviving animals. Once killed and butchered some of the buffalo were roasted on the spot as an immediate reward for the hunters.

Métis hunters often employed a third method of buffalo hunting known as running the herd. Scouts would locate a herd and the hunters would ride toward the animals in formation. At a signal the herd would be stampeded and horsemen would ride through the melee shooting prime cows as they swept by them. Again and again the hunters would ride into the herd and shoot their prey until a sufficient number of animals had been taken (Sealey and Lussier, 1975: 24). It was important to own a highly-trained buffalo pony when running the herd and they were very valuable animals. A well-trained pony knew which side of the buffalo to pursue (left-side), and get in close enough so the rider could shoot at a strategic spot and wound or kill the buffalo. The chase was accomplished without the rider having to hold onto the pony's reins because his mount knew just where to go.

When the hunt was over and the carts were loaded to capacity, they would form a single file and head home. The caravan followed an established order of march. At the head was the caravan master who travelled in a covered wagon, followed by the male adults, each walking ahead of his rig and in step with the leaders. The family baggage was loaded on top where the women also rode, and the younger people walked alongside the carts or rode their ponies, tending livestock that occasionally accompanied the procession (Pelletier, 1977: 33).

The hunt itself was governed by very strict regulations. There was to be no hunting on Sunday and no one was to lag behind, dash ahead, or break from their group. No one could shoot until the order was given, and each captain and his followers were to provide night patrols to guard the camp. Severe punishments were meted out to violators. For a first offence, one's saddle and bridle were cut up; the second offence was punished by having one's coat cut up, and for a third offence, the violator was publicly flogged. Assembled hunters had a voice in making these rules as a means of added assurance in making them binding (Purich, 1988: 30).

A typical hunting expedition drew large groups of people. During a mid-nineteenth century hunt, for example, the hunt from the Red River settlement involved 620 men, 650 women, 360 children, and 1 210 Red River carts, and covered an area equal to that of a modern city (Sprenger, 1978: 116).

A fourth approach to buffalo hunting was the sneakup. When hunters spotted a nearby herd, they would often drape themselves in buffalo robes and crawl over to the herd, mimicking buffalo actions. When the time was right they would take out an animal with bow and arrow and remain as quiet as they could. Often several animals could be killed in this manner without stampeding the herd. At times winter camps were chosen on the basis of their proximity to wintering buffalo herds so the sneakup method could be employed.

It is anybody's guess as to how many buffalo were terminated during these buffalo hunts. Estimates are hard to come by, but guessed numbers suggest that as many as one hundred thousand buffalo were killed by the Métis in a single season. Estimates vary, but there were probably as many as 40 million buffalo on the Canadian prairies during 1780-1810 and their numbers were increasing. Records indicate that even as late as 1873, a single herd of buffalo of immense numbers was sighted in the Cypress Hills area along what is now the southern Alberta-Saskatchewan border. Apparently one party rode 150 miles (240 kilometres) in one week and never lost sight of a buffalo herd. In 1883, however, only ten years later, there were less than one thousand buffalo left on the prairies, predominantly located in parks and on private reserves (Sealey and Lussier, 1975: 230).

The end of an exciting hunt always meant a lot of work for the women who were responsible for butchering. The meat was hauled into temporary camps where it was cut into thin slabs and hung on drying racks. Later it was made into pemmican by being beaten with sticks or stones and mixed with hot buffalo fat and berries. Generally, additives to pemmican were avoided because their inclusion was directly proportionate to the speed of spoilage. The prepared pemmican mixture was poured into buffalo bags weighing about one hundred pounds (45 kilograms) each and the mouth of the bag was sewed up and sealed with tallow. The contents were then pressed into a flat shape about six or seven inches (15-18 centimetres) thick. These evenly sized sacks of food could be piled like rows of little logs or packed into tight corners for travelling.

Pemmican could be stored for years and although it was quite tasteless it provided sufficient daily nutrition. While the buffalo provided the base for pemmican-making, the meat of other animals such as deer, elk, moose, and caribou was also used. A boon to the hunter or long-distance traveller, pemmican was virtually indispensable on the Canadian plains. It was also a compact food; one pound (about half a kilogram) of pemmican was equivalent to three or four pounds of fresh meat in food value. Some tribes, like the Blackfoot, used less fat in their recipe and translated a pound of pemmican into the nourishment of five pounds of fresh meat (McHugh, 1972: 89). Though the First Nations cultures thrived on it, the demise of pemmican was eventually influenced by its lack of flavor, thanks to newly-emerging forms of diet in North America and the disdain for it voiced by the nonNative sector of North American society.

In 1868 another buffalo hunt-related practice was initiated, that of gathering buffalo bones for sale to fertilizer companies. Buffalo bones were used for manufacturing phosphate fertilizers as well as for making charcoal filters used in refining sugar (MacEwan, 1995: 167). The Métis were active in this trade and many saw the enterprise as an Aboriginal right. Using their famous Red River carts, they scoured the prairies in search of bison bones. Money obtained from the sale of bones was used to pay for groceries, tobacco,

Epsom salts, clothing, and even medicine such as Dr. Bell's Medical Wonder. At the very least buffalo bone hunting gave the Métis access to another needed, albeit temporary, means of income.

Cultural Transitions

The beginning of the nineteenth century posed a potential crossroads experience before members of the Red River community. The wealth of the fur trade was diminishing and prices were falling on the European market. The North West Company was in severe danger of failure until Thomas Douglas, Earl of Selkirk, a local landowner, induced his relatives to buy a controlling interest in the company at a bargain price. Selkirk was personally committed to forming colonies for Scotsmen in Canada since 1803, and having done so successfully in Prince Edward Island, he now set his sights on the Red River Colony. His compatriots arrived in 1812 with few possessions, and faced a harsh winter with little time to prepare for it. Of even more concern was the presence of the Nor'Westers (affiliates of the North West Company), who interfered with the developmental plans of the invaders. It was thus decided in collaboration with the governor, Miles Macdonell, that the Red River settlement be dismantled and new colonies formed that would be more representative of the interests of the Hudson's Bay Company (Lower, 1977: 151f). In the ten year period between 1809 and 1819 a total of 450 000 acres (182 186 hectares) of land were taken away from Métis tenants, by government order, and turned over to incoming settlers.

By 1811, two boatloads of Scottish immigrants were on their way to take up residence in the Red River Colony area to validate Selkirk's claims for a new civilization. Local Métis supplied game and garden produce for the new dwellers who probably would have starved the first winter if it had not been for Métis assistance. Within two years, however, the scene changed, and the Métis became very opposed to the establishment of a colony of infiltrators. Their stance was partially aided by the attitude of the colony governor, Miles Macdonell, who refused to acknowledge the legitimacy of the prior existence of the Métis settlement and did not regard the Métis as his cultural equal.

A potential conflict situation was influenced by the presence of the two major fur trading companies in the area, the Hudson's Bay Company and the North West Company. Company spokesmen took opposing views on the role of the culturally-mixed evolving settlement. The Hudson's Bay Company saw an advantage in encouraging a strong European presence because Scottish immigrants had experience in railway building, the military, and other related interests. The North West Company, on the other hand, saw the foreign presence as a threat to the continuance of the fur trade. The success of this settlement would undoubtedly encourage others, and soon an alternate lifestyle in Canada would become evident. As the North West Company leaders saw it, it would be best to influence the Métis to make a strong stand for their cultural heritage and land rights and ward off any kind of campaign to the contrary from Miles Macdonell's followers (Purich, 1988: 34).

Seven Oaks

On instigation from a North West spokesman, Alexander Macdonell (no relation to Miles Macdonell), a plan was elaborated to deliberately destroy the Scottish stronghold at Red River. With Alexander Macdonell's encouragement, the Métis selected Cuthbert Grant as their military general. As an indication of how unusual loyalties develop, Grant was the son of a wealthy Scottish trader for the North West Company, but he chose to be loyal to his Métis roots. He was well-educated, articulate and sophisticated; on his other side, it was reported that he was a braggart and a ladies' man (five wives in the space of a decade).

The first measures against the Selkirk community encouraged by Grant were designed to ensure discomfort to its residents by threats of invasion and attack (Lower, 1977: 152). This worked to some extent so that a number of newcomers soon moved to Upper Canada to avoid possible conflict. The governor of the colony retaliated and ordered that no Métis would henceforth be allowed to run buffalo in the area, and he ordered his men to seize the Métis food supplies of pemmican which had been stored at Fort La Souris.

Terrorism was the next chosen weapon, and it became manifest in the form of burning crops, stealing cattle, and horses, and machinery, and destroying fences and buildings (Purich, 1988: 36). Eventually, enough settlers left for Upper Canada so that the antagonists considered the settlement permanently dismantled. A quick turn of events occurred, in 1815, however, when a new governor, Robert Semple, was dispatched to the area but he served for only one year. Semple was an aggressive leader, determined to serve his company well. As legal representative of the Hudson's Bay Company, he took it upon himself to determine the exact nature of Métis activities and acted accordingly. Quickly he arrested the leader of the North West post at Fort Gibraltar, Duncan Cameron, and forced a show-down of military strength. When he heard about the Métis capturing Hudson's Bay Company pemmican boats he took a company of 20 men and accosted a group of 15 Métis face-to-face. Although he was warned that a larger army of Métis was nearby, he threatened the group with severe action if they did not desist. Purich describes the later events in this manner:

> The two groups met in a shady group of trees known as Seven Oaks in the later afternoon of June 19 [1816]. Grant sent a messenger offering the governor a choice–either surrender or be fired upon. The messenger and Semple spoke briefly and Semple tried to grab the messenger's gun and reins; the messenger fell from his horse and started to run; shots were exchanged. Both sides went into action. By nightfall twenty-one settlers, including Semple himself, and one Métis were dead. (Purich, 1988: 37)

This event was recorded in the annals of Canadian history as the infamous Battle of Seven Oaks which occurred on the northern limits of the present City of Winnipeg (Lower, 1977: 152). The confrontation did not resolve the situation, because when Selkirk heard that deaths had occurred, he recruited soldiers from Swiss regiments that had recently disbanded in Canada after the War of 1812, seized the post at Fort William, and charged the North West Company with the most serious and premeditated of crimes. He also issued a warrant for the arrest of General Grant, and when Grant voluntarily went to Montreal to face charges, he was released on bail and returned to the west. Court proceedings against him were abandoned and he was subsequently hired by the Hudson's Bay Company (Purich, 1988, 38).

Selkirk continued on to Red River in the spring of 1817, restored order, and reestablished his colony. He then set about obtaining legal action against the North West Company, but as Lower notes, their influence in high places was so strong that his accusations were met with counter-accusations until ". . . it became plain that there was no justice to be obtained against a Nor'Wester in a Canadian court" (Lower, 1977: 153). Selkirk appealed to the English courts as well, but the influence of the North West Company reached into the depths of the British Colonial office. Selkirk also tried to obtain the cooperation of several First Nations such as local Ojibwa, Crees, and Assiniboines in a battle against the Métis by signing treaties with them. Eventually Selkirk lost his health and his money and died a defeated man. His colony, however, continued to thrive, but so did the Métis community who flew their first flag with a renewed sense of pride and vigour.

Company Merger

Finally, in 1821 the North West Company and the Hudson's Bay Company merged, with some substantial effect on the operation of the fur trade. The rivalry of the two companies was evident in the duplicate trading posts spread across the country, from the Great Lakes to the Pacific, and from the Red River to the Arctic. In reality, however, this action was not an amalgamation, but simply a takeover by the Hudson's Bay Company. English power dominated, and the Canadian company had little choice but to buckle under. The long haul from Montreal, the expense of the court proceedings against Lord Selkirk, the vigorous counter-strokes by the Hudson's Bay Company, and discontent among company employees had taken their toll on the North West Company. Faced by the outcome of the events of 1885, company officials were forced to accept its defeat. Its leaders tried hard to support the efforts of the missionaries to gain recognition from the Métis, but it was not to be.

The subsequent influence of the Hudson's Bay Company was profound, and their philosophy persisted in the new management style that developed. As time went on, the nature of Red River community life changed dramatically. By 1821, the Red River settlement became a haven for retired Hudson's Bay Company employees. It had been a condition agreed to by Lord Selkirk back in 1811 that one-tenth of the area granted to him would be reserved for "any persons being or having been in the service of the said Governor and Company for a term of not less than three years" (Stanley, 1963: 7). By the following year it was estimated there were no fewer than 200 clerks and employees in the community.

In the course of time, the Native population of Red River also increased and cross-cultural marriages continued. The Métis settlement dwellers manifested a variety of vocations in their repertoire including buffalo hunting, fishing, agriculture, freighting, and working in an adjunct capacity with the fur trade (Friesen, 1985). A half century later (1871), historians would record that the population of Red River comprised 5 720 Métis, 4 080 English-speaking Breeds, and 1 600 white settlers (Stanley, 1963: 8). The present cultural diversity so evident in the make-up of the modern City of Winnipeg bears testimony to its strong multicultural antecedents, now much more than a century old.

The culture of the two dominant interracial groups in Red River grew to be quite different from one another. Obviously, the language of their fathers, English-speaking and French-speaking, was a major difference, but religion also played a role. Those of Scottish heritage inherited a generous portion of Presbyterian Calvinism, with its strong orientation to work, and a quest for virtue, both accompanied by a preponderance of guilt. The French Métis, on the other hand, were described by the Scots as "frivolous, reckless and vain" (Stanley, 1963: 9). The French Métis claimed and professed their religion (mostly through behavior, rather than testimony), but did not allow it to dictate their every thought or action. They saw no virtue in work for its own sake, and they regarded themselves as a free people who were prepared to defend their rights.

Lest this record depict Red River life as idyllic, there were also political issues with which to contend, but Métis victories in these events simply served to enhance their feelings of peoplehood and put the fear of God into the hearts of their opponents. Governor George Simpson, who arrived in 1821, saw the Métis as a political guard to be reckoned with. They were also a strong military force which was demonstrated in their defeat of the highly-regaled Sioux to the south in order to assure the safe travel of Métis traders who peddled "illicit trade goods" in St. Paul, Minnesota. Simpson had tried to stop this form of trade, but he was never able to obtain sufficient troops to end this form of Canadian-United States "free trade" (McLean, 1985: 13).

Colony government became a key issue after Lord Selkirk's death when the administration of the Red River community property was turned over to the Douglas family. In 1836, the family relinquished this control and gave it back to the Hudson's Bay Company. The Company appointed governors over the area and councils were set up. The first French-speaking Métis were given a seat on council for the first time in 1853, but in the years that followed, both halfbreeds and Métis were awarded substantially more recognition in the matter of appointments (Stanley, 1963: 10). In the interim, however, several issues drove the Métis towards seeking a greater recognition of their rightful place in Red River operations.

Earlier, in 1835, the Hudson's Bay Company enacted legislation forbidding Native and nonNative marriages in regard to their employees. These regulations prohibited male employees from initiating relationships with Native women and from making permanent economic arrangements for them, or for any children born to such unions in the event of a separation of the family. The legislation served to keep more families together after retirement, and added an element of stability to the communities surrounding the Red River Colony. Within 20 years, however, about 80 percent of the colony's population was Métis (Lussier and Sealey, 1978: Vol. 2: 110-111). They soon comprised the dominant population in the community thereby gradually reduced the incidence of intermarriage. Fewer immigrants were arriving from Europe at this time, and the resentment towards the minority of nonNatives who governed local affairs grew in intensity (Friesen, 1985).

The Sayer Incident

In 1849, the Métis at Red River broke the trade monopoly of the Hudson's Bay Company by forcing the Recorder of the court to acquit Guillaume Sayer, a Métis charged with breaching company regulations. It was another in a series of politically-related moves that served to establish the phenomenon of Métis identity in the history of Canada. As a way to save face on the part of the nonNative powerbrokers, the jury returned a verdict of guilty with a strong recommendation for mercy. This was supported by the Hudson's Bay Company factor and Sayer was dismissed with an admonition.

Technically the company's authority had been upheld, but no one in the colony believed that it could any longer be enforced. A local publication, founded ten years earlier and appropriately named, *The Nor'Wester,* gave its own account of the event and repudiated the role of the Hudson's Bay Company as a form of government. The paper suggested that territories controlled by the Hudson's Bay Company should now be turned over to the new Canadian government.

On December 1, 1869 it was decreed that lands under control of the Hudson's Bay Company should indeed be transferred to the Canadian government. Negotiations had been conducted in London, England, but no one thought much about consulting the Métis. The Métis worried some about becoming part of Canada, partially because they feared such a move would signal a welcome to people wanting to immigrate west from Ontario and thus upset the balance of power between Native and nonNative populations.

In order to defend their interests, the Métis formed a National Committee of the Métis of Red River with John Bruce as president and Louis Riel as secretary. They refused to allow the new governor-designate, William McDougall, to visit with them until they had opportunity to discuss their plans with Ottawa. McDougall then issued a proclamation on December 1, 1869, declaring the transfer complete (Flanagan, 1979a: 82-89). Although he had been warned in a letter by Prime Minister John A. Macdonald not to do so, but the prime minister's letter had apparently not arrived by the date of the announcement. In response to his announcement, on December 8, 1869, the Métis declared a Provisional Government under a specially drawn-up Bill of Rights (Lussier and Sealey, 1978, Vol. 1: 21-22). Louis Riel became president later that month. The die was cast; the Métis were on their way.

Conclusion

A century passed before Métis land claims were given serious consideration. The 1970s witnessed an enhanced amount of increased activity among Canada's ethnic minorities as each attempted to gain a wider audience in the nation's mainstream. A number of Métis organizations became prominent on the political scene, some of them witnessing an amalgamation of nonStatus and Métis interests. The move towards Métis self-government was also accentuated although it has been seriously hindered by the lack of land base, impeding government protocol, and public disinterest. Meanwhile, Métis cultural development is on course featuring its own unique history, values, norms, beliefs, and behaviors. The political efforts of the Congress of Aboriginal Peoples, supplemented by such associations as the Métis National Council and a host of provincial Métis organizations, the Métis voice will undoubtedly continue to be heard across the land. Perhaps in the near future they will attain the national recognition they deserve as a founding people. As Shore and Barkwell (1997: 232) note:

> . . . it should be remembered that the Manitoba Métis Federation has retained, as one of its major objectives since its founding in 1967, the reintegration of the Métis People into the Province that they founded over one hundred and twenty-five years ago.

4

Initiator

I know that through the grace of God I am the founder of Manitoba. – Louis Riel, defence speech, Regina, SK, on July 31, 1885 (Colombo, 1987: 327).

For ninety years now Riel has remained one of the perennially fascinating figures in Canadian history, and not only among French Canadians. He has been the subject of histories, biographies, poems, plays, and at least one opera: the object of execration, contempt, controversy, analysis, pity, and reverence. – George Woodcock. Author of *Gabriel Dumont: The Métis Chief and His Lost World*, (1976: 8)

The lives of very few Canadians have been as controversially depicted in the Canadian historical record as that of Louis Riel. Despised and belittled by government leaders and bureaucrats, and admired by his people, no one can deny the impact of his actions on the Canadian west. Ironically, Riel's death in 1885 probably did more for his cause than anything he accomplished throughout his lifetime. There is ample evidence to indicate that the ripple effect of his undertakings is rapidly forming ever larger circles of impact.

It would be presumptuous to attempt yet another indepth treatment of the life and impact of Louis Riel since several of his biographers have many times painstakingly and adequately covered the subject (Stanley, 1963; Bowsfield, 1971; Howard, 1974; Charlebois, 1975; Flanagan, 1979a; Sprague, 1988; Braz, 2003). Nevertheless, in this context it would be negligent not to mention the salient points of Riel's life and career or fail to pinpoint the more significant and controversial aspects of this Canadian hero.

In one sense Louis Riel was a man before his time; he held to a concept of nationhood for the Métis which now, more than a century later, is being revived. Riel saw the Métis not only as a nation but as natives of a country, just like their English halfbreed cousins. According to Riel, it was through Métis descent from First Nations ancestors that his people shared Aboriginal title to the land. Thus they had both a moral and legal right to compensation from the state in return for the extinguishment of that title (Flanagan, 1979b, 121).

Early Life

Louis Riel Jr. was born at St. Boniface (a prairie settlement) on October 22, 1844, to a family who could trace their ancestry back to the closing days of the seventeenth century. Following his parents' biological lineage indicates that Riel was one-eighth Indian, but born and raised in a distinctly French cultural configuration (Dobbin, n.d.: 18-19). On this basis it is necessary to make note of Louis Riel's unique personal journey which led him to the front lines of the Métis movement.

The story, in brief, begins with the career of Louis Riel Sr. who was a miller when his eldest son Louis, was born, and who encouraged the future reformer to take up formal studies. As a result, for ten years young Riel studied humanities, law, and the classics, and even considered a call to church ministry. Eventually he took up employment with a law firm and thus met many active and aspiring politicians including Wilfred Laurier who later became Canada's Prime Minister. In 1866, after a brief engagement to a young woman of breeding, Marie-Julie Guernon, whose family objected to Riel's Native ancestry, the two separated and Riel lost interest in his studies. He then spent some time in the Métis settlements in the Red River area of southern Manitoba, and there his search for collegiality in his commiseration paid off, and he soon found himself at the forefront of the Métis cause.

Louis Riel, the eldest of eleven children, was baptized on the day of his birth by Bishop, Mgr. Norbert Provencher, the same priest who had married the Louis' parents a year earlier. After some years of work experience in various capacities, Riel began to call himself Louis "David" Riel, possibly in hopes of identifying with the biblical hero of that name (Flanagan, 1979b). Riel was named after his father, and grew up in a house on the Seine River near present-day Winnipeg. Riel's ancestry, not surprisingly, included fur traders and trappers whose lifestyles were interrupted by the establishment of Selkirk's people at Red River. Riel's maternal grandmother, Marie-Anne Gaboury, who was born in Quebec (Lower Canada), packed and paddled her share of the couple's belongings over rough portages. The family finally settled in Red River where Marie-Anne's husband, Jean-Baptiste Lagimodiere, was granted title to a strip of land along the Red River opposite Fort Douglas. It was here that their daughter, Julie Lagimodiere (the future mother of Louis Riel, Jr.), was born (Charlebois, 1975).

Julie Lagimodiere was raised in the Red River settlement among the Métis. She grew up to become a young woman of strong faith, and she initially turned down Riel Sr.'s proposal of marriage because she felt destined to become a nun. Seeking direction in prayer, she saw a vision of an old man surrounded by flames "whose deep voice commanded her to follow the will of her parents" (Stanley, 1963: 2). Convinced that she had heard the voice of God, she married Riel on January 21, 1844, in the Cathedral of St. Boniface. A discrepancy of dates concerning the date of their marriage exists because Julie was embarrassed by the fact that her first child was born just nine months after their wedding. To disguise this fact she allegedly told her children that she and their father had been married a year earlier than they were (Flanagan, 1979a: 4).

Louis Riel Sr. grew up in Lower Canada and learned the trade of a wool carder. At the age of 21 he joined the Hudson's Bay Company and worked at Rainy River. He lived with a Métis woman in a common-law relation for a while and fathered a daughter by her (Flanagan, 1979a: 1). In 1842 he quit his job and joined the Oblate Order to become a priest. A few months later, having changed his mind about his Divine calling, he was back at his Hudson's Bay post, met Julie Lagimodiere, fell in love, and married her. He engaged unsuccessfully in farming for a time, then came to the conclusion that the economic rewards from this enterprise were too limited for him. Perhaps it was because he felt inferior to the Lagimodieres, who were one of the most prominent families of St. Boniface, that he was motivated to "shop around for a bit" for a more lucrative occupation. Subsequently, he operated a grist mill, a fulling mill, and a carding mill on the Seine River.

It has been speculated that the inspiration for Louis Riel Jr.'s later mission originated at least partially in his parents' orientation to life. The elder Riel was a restless and ambitious soul who played a memorable role in the Métis uprising of 1849 involving 300 armed Métis who tried to break the monopoly of the Hudson's Bay Company. The Sayer incident, mentioned earlier, resulted in four Métis being charged by the company. Guillaume Sayer himself was discharged without punishment because the court recommended leniency. This action was undoubtedly motivated by political reasons, since the Métis in the area had become a very capable military force.

Although only five years old at the time, the younger Riel apparently savored memories of his father's political activities and sometimes considered his own mission as an extension of his father's work. Coupled with this sense of continuity, as Flanagan notes (1979a: 5), Riel may also have been motivated by the fact of his father's marginal economic position in the community which he felt he could remedy through political ambition.

Riel's mother, Julie, may also have inspired him towards high achievement, especially through her commitment to religious principles. She encouraged her son always to heed the Divine voice of God. According to his own testimony, ". . . her devotion to her religious obligations always left me with the deepest impression of her good example" (Bowsfield, 1971: 17). Julie sent her son to the Grey Sisters for his schooling, and even though their school had been designed as an all-girls' school, Louis was admitted. In 1854 the Right Reverend Bishop Alexandre Tache, first Bishop of St. Boniface, encouraged the Christian Brothers to begin a boys' school so Louis was transferred there.

Riel was a good student, and was one of four boys chosen to begin the study of Latin in a new school at Fort Garry with Father Lefloch. Since his parents were unable to pay for his schooling, Bishop Tache found a willing and generous patron in the person of Joseph Masson of Terrebonne. The Masson family had amassed a sizable fortune and designated some of their money to finance the education of young Métis lads selected by Bishop Tache. After

Joseph Masson's death his widow, Sophie, continued to provide this form of benevolence.

On June 1, 1858, Louis Riel and two of his peers travelled east to Montreal via Minnesota. At St. Paul they met with Riel's father, Louis Sr., who was freighting trade goods from the United States via Red River. This was the last time Riel saw his father who died before Louis returned to Red River (Charlebois, 1975: 18). Riel stayed in Montreal and studied at the College of the Sulpician Fathers (Seminaire de St. Sulpice), the oldest college in the city. He boarded at the college and thus was afforded the opportunity to rub shoulders with individuals from the upper echelons of society. He learned good manners and social polish and made several acquaintances whose modelling later aided him in his political climb.

Riel did well in his studies and considered his training a time of testing. The curriculum included Latin, Greek, mathematics, philosophy, and theology, and required rigorous study on the part of students. Louis eagerly obeyed the rules of the institution and tried to discipline himself as an appropriate trainee for the prieshood. In February, 1864, Riel was informed of his father's death and he was so affected that his studies faltered. He missed classes and complained of illness. The following year he left the seminary.

Riel's next step was to become a student-at-law in the office of the famous leader, Rodolphe Laflamme, of the Rouge Party in Quebec. Laflamme had also been a student at the seminary and subsequently became both a student of and a companion to Louis-Joseph Papineau who was an early leader of the Revolution of 1837. Later Papineau became a successful politician.

Riel found a sharp contrast of values and procedures between political life and seminary life. The theme of all major activity was Quebec nationalism, and it is possible that Riel's vision for the birth of a Métis nation was at least partially whetted during this period. There is speculation that he might have been happy at this career, but two factors changed his destiny. The first was the death of his father and Riel's resultant conviction that he should return west to help his mother. The second was the collapse of his brief engagement with a young women, Marie-Julie Guernon, of Mile End, who broke off the relationship because her parents were opposed to their daughter marrying a Métis (MacEwan, 1981). Riel and Marie-Julie signed a prenuptial agreement on June 12, 1866, which stated that there would be a separation of property in the event of a dissolution of the marriage. The agreement also specified that neither partner would be responsible for the other's debts in the event of marriage breakdown, and Riel gave up any right to a dowry from the bride's side (Flanagan, 1979a: 24). Despite this concession on Riel's part, Guernon's parents objected to the marriage and on June 19, 1866, the two parted and Louis Riel left permanently for the west.

Western Sojourn

Little is known of the early years of Riel's sojourn in the west except that he lived for nearly two years in Chicago, then in St. Paul, Minnesota, where he worked in a dry goods store. He arrived at his mother's home in St. Boniface on July 28, 1868, just 24 years old and without specific goals as to his future (Bowsfield, 1971). When he settled in Red River, Riel found himself in a very different colony from that which he had left a decade before. The Métis were living in an increasingly smaller and more desperate world, much beset by English hatred and uncertainty as to the future. Even their own society had become stratified with more and more goods accruing to the wealthy Métis merchant farmers of St. Boniface, St. Vital, and St. Norbert. It bothered Riel that their wealth was based on the success of the local grain market and the lucrative St. Paul freight contracts with no input from the labor force. The majority of Métis workers squatted along the banks of the Red and Assiniboine Rivers and were in constant competition for the declining resources of the plains and the river lots (Pannekoek, 1979: 69).

Perhaps the worst calamity at the time was drought. During the summer of 1868, grasshoppers devoured all growing crops and the Red River community was faced an immediate famine. Some settlers swallowed their pride and appealed to communities in eastern Canada and the United States for provisions. Obviously affected by drought conditions, buffalo herds began to graze further away from the settlements (MacEwan,1981: 75).

Besides physical changes in buildings and industries in his home community, Riel encountered significant political changes. A year earlier Canada had become a nation, but the event was accomplished without any input from the west. In the interim to these events, Western Canadians had become used to looking to the south, to Minnesota specifically, for economic advantage. The Red River settlement was set for a change in administration to local control because residents were no longer satisfied to be governed by the Select Committee in London, England. Newcomers who migrated to the community questioned the authority of the Hudson's Bay Company and refused to obey its orders. The newspaper, the *Nor'Wester,* reported all the complaints of disillusioned citizens and recommended a stronger alliance with the Canada of the east. The paper also agitated for an open and elected form of administration and fostered an air of desperation in its campaign.

The response of the Canadian government to the cries of the west was to announce the building of a road from Fort Garry, Manitoba, to Lake of the Woods, Ontario. The road was seen to be necessary for the development of the west in order to provide a better means of communication and exchange. In the fall of 1869 a surveyor, John A. Snow, and a small party of assistants arrived in Red River to map out the road. The Hudson's Bay Company which laid claim to the land protested, but allowed the work to proceed. Snow's party initially began their work at Oak Point, Manitoba, a small Métis settlement, but it was soon charged that Snow underpaid his men and often overcharged them for provisions which he issued in place of wages (Stanley, 1963; 51).

In effect Snow's mandate was regarded with disdain by local residents and it was rumored that the purpose of the roadway was to flood the west with ambitious and dominating eastern immigrants who would forever change their relaxed and unhurried way of life. In addition, the opening up of railway lines, particularly in the United States, aided in the rapid demise of the buffalo. Everyone, it seemed, suddenly wanted to kill buffalo for hides, for sport, or merely for the novelty of it. In fact, thousands of animals were slaughtered for their tongues alone, which was a delicacy for the hunters. New repeating rifles also made the hunt much more successful because with such a gun one hunter could kill dozens of animals on a single mission (Stanley, 1963: 233). This was the new west to which Louis Riel was returning; it was one in which he was not sure he had a part to play.

When news of unrest in the Métis community reached the offices of Hudson's Bay Company officials the administration immediately sought a means by which to protect their interests. On December 22, 1868, the Department Governor of the Hudson's Bay Company wrote to Sir Frederic Rogers of the Colonial Office requesting the intervention of Her Majesty's government in what was termed a threefold trespass upon the freehold territory of the Company. The correspondence was forwarded to William McDougall in England whose task it became to acquire Rupert's land from the Hudson's Bay Company (Charlebois, 1975: 33). Louis Riel was probably the first Métis in the west to learn about McDougall's new responsibility, because of his prior experience in Montreal. In an attempt to formalize their objections, on October 16, 1869, a group of Métis met at Father Ritchot's home in St. Norbert where they elected John Bruce as their first president and Louis Riel as secretary of the "National Committee of Métis." They also designed and adopted a new flag.

On October 30, 1869, William McDougall arrived in the border-town of Pembina, Manitoba, travelling via the United States. He was greeted by a messenger who handed him an order prepared by the new National Committee of Métis, and ordered not to enter the territory without permission of the committee. At first McDougall was annoyed, and travelled to an abandoned Hudson's Bay post a few miles north of the border. There an armed Métis patrol of fourteen riflemen ordered him to leave the country by "order of the government." As he left for the United States he was instructed not to return to Manitoba territory (Charlebois, 1975: 39).

William McDougall's political negotiating philosophy was clearly out of touch with the times. He believed that anyone who issued an order in the name of the Queen should be obeyed, even if that person did not have official sanction. Riel, as a spokesperson for the Métis, believed only that the Queen was simply a woman who was rich enough to buy the furs which were his livelihood. Despite this lack of respect for the monarchy, he was willing to negotiate with the Queen's representatives, albeit from a strong political base.

On November 2, 1869, Riel moved on Fort Garry with an army of 400 men and tried to secure the cooperation of local English-speaking settlers. He invited them to attend a meeting to elect governing representatives because the National Committee of Métis had expelled the governing council. Much of the substance of the subsequent meeting resulted in a debate between Riel and James Ross, a former editor of the *Nor'Wester* who saw Riel's efforts to protect the people as little more than a selfish act of egotism.

On December 1, 1869, two historically significant events occurred simultaneously. William McDougall, with a few followers, crossed the border to an abandoned fort north of Pembina and declared that the fort was now Canadian territory. Then he scurried back to the United States for safety. At the same time, Riel, as secretary of the National Committee of Métis, formulated a list of rights that included the right to elect and organize their own legislation, the right to claim a portion of land to be appropriated for the erection of schools, and the right to build bridges, roads, and public buildings (Charlebois, 1975: 44).

William McDougall's ill-famed proclamation was denounced by Canadian authorities on the grounds that he had used the Queen's name without permission, and risked military actions which might have embarrassed Her Majesty. Moreover, Prime Minister John Macdonald washed his hands of any responsibility in the matter, remarking that McDougall had done pretty well everything he could to destroy the government's chances ". . . of an amicable settlement with these wild people" (Howard, 1974: 146).

One of the acts for which Louis Riel's name has been immortalized in the minds of many Métis people had occurred a few weeks earlier, on October 11, 1869, when John Snow's road surveyors arrived to begin their work. Because the Métis felt that the Canadian government had no right to make surveys on Métis lands without the express permission of the people, the work was stopped when Riel stepped on the survey chain and proclaimed, "You shall go no further" (Davidson, 1955: 29). The surveyors were so surprised by Riel's action that they hastily consulted amongst themselves, packed their equipment, and left the area. No violence erupted.

On December 13, 1869, William McDougall returned to Ottawa, having failed to get a response from Riel whom he had tried to contact. In the meantime, John Bruce resigned as president of the National Committee of Métis and Riel took over the position. As leader of the new organization, Riel took it upon himself to function as the head of what he saw as a developing state. The rights and responsibilities of the new state included arresting and taking prisoners for insurrection against the provisional government. In due course this situation worked against Riel, particularly in the taking of one Thomas Scott as prisoner. Scott was an Orangeman, and completely loyal to the Crown to the nth degree. He was outspoken, and given to a lifestyle of recklessness, stubbornness, and lawlessness. When imprisoned and finally threatened with the death penalty, he taunted his captors crying, "The Métis (sic) are a pack of cowards. They will not dare to shoot me" (Stanley, 1963: 112). Riel himself said that Scott was a troublesome character, incorrigible, and a ringleader of rebellion. Perhaps he made these observations to justify meting out the death penalty, an action with which he himself was not quite comfortable. Still, Riel had to appease his own critics who might have suggested that he was going soft. Undoubtedly, the execution of Thomas Scott became the most controversial of Louis Riel's actions and, as some critics have suggested, ultimately his downfall. He justified the action by saying that the Métis must make Canada respect the new provincial government.

On March 4, 1870, Thomas Scott was executed by a firing squad.

Unsuccessful Campaign

On March 23, 1870, two delegates of the newly-formed provisional government of Red River, Father Ritchot and Alfred Scott, left for Ottawa to negotiate a possible union with Canada. The upshot of the negotiations was that Father Ritchot was able to obtain most of the rights demanded by the Métis because Prime Minister John A. Macdonald feared a loss of support from the French in Quebec if he resisted. Unfortunately Macdonald's verbal promise to Father Richot was not put into writing, and as the new Manitobans soon found out, when push came to shove, it meant nothing. In fact, Macdonald chose to employ troops to "keep the peace in the west," and since Canada had virtually no troops of her own the prime minister obtained British permission to employ that country's troops. Macdonald's request implied that the Red River community was the target of restless Métis and American annexationists who were embroiled in political disputes. Colonel Garnet Wolseley was selected by government military channels to lead the Red River Expedition which left Toronto on May 21, 1870.

Riel saw no reason not to welcome British troops into his territory since they allegedly came on behalf of Canadian government leaders who signalled that Wolseley's mission was one of peace. Although he knew differently, Wolseley did not publicly announce the purpose of his travel to Red River residents, but eventually word leaked to Riel that this not a mission of peace but a potential military action. It was reported that Wolseley hoped Riel would bolt when he heard that military representatives of the Canadian government were on their way but that did not happen. Wolseley and his men surrounded Fort Garry, and despite their hardest efforts to do so, could not locate Louis Riel. Wolseley remarked that he was glad about Riel's embarkment, suggesting that he would have hung Riel if he had not fled.

Wolseley's "peace-keeping" mission resulted in the sentencing of several individuals involved in the execution of Thomas Scott even though their deaths could not directly be linked to the actions of Wolseley's troops. When Wolseley took command, those residents who had supported the establishment of the provisional government were treated like enemies of the Canadian government. Riel, in the meantime, fled to the safety of the United States where he and two others drew up a petition addressed to United States President Ulysses Simpson Grant requesting his intercession with Queen Victoria on behalf of the Métis. Riel rejected the arguments of the annexationists that it would be a good time to negotiate the annexation of the Canadian prairies to United States. Riel perceived the prairies as a separate and special place for the occupation of people of Métis ancestry only.

Riel's exile in the United States was partially motivated by the fact that a price of $5 000 had been placed on his head by the Province of Ontario. His friends warned him that various members of the federal army had also threatened his life. Despite his absence from the country, Riel was thrice elected to and thrice expelled from the Canadian House of Commons. His expulsion was met with lively debate as, for example, on April 9, 1874, when it was moved that Riel should be expelled because he had fled from justice and had failed to take his place in the Canadian legislature (Charlebois, 1975: 105). One of Riel's supporters was young Wilfred Laurier (later to become prime minister), who sat in the House of Commons for the first time. Laurier argued that Riel should not be regarded as a rebel because his only crime had been to raise the national flag in another part of the country, hardly an act of treason. Laurier regretted the Thomas Scott incident and suggested that if that event had not occurred, events at Red River might have constituted a glorious page in Canadian history (Bowsfield, 1971: 71). Prime Minister John A. Macdonald stated that he would not recognize the Red River delegates and did not perceive their election as an issue to be discussed on the floor of the house.

To sum up, interpretations of the events of 1869-1870 in western Canada are manifold. Five of the most popular include these descriptions: (i) a French-English conflict; (ii) civilization versus frontier; (iii) a civil war; (iv) a conspiracy of the Catholic clergy; and, (v) a social, political and religious reaction to rapidly changing conditions (Lussier, 1979: 12). With the advantage of hindsight it would obviously be foolhardy to opt for anything other than a multidimensional interpretation of the events that transpired.

In 1878, Louis Riel dared to return to Red River from exile. The area was now attracting immigrants from Quebec and Ontario (Orangemen) and from various parts of Europe. Missionaries arrived who tried to assist the Métis in becoming farmers and gardeners now that hunting buffalo was no longer a viable lifestyle. Few Native residents were able to cultivate the land successfully since they had no previous experience as farmers, equipment was scarce, or they were too poor to purchase it, and the instruction they received was less than adequate (Bowsfield, 1971: 99). The influx of newcomers motivated many Métis to relocate to

Saskatchewan, particularly to the northern areas, while others migrated south to the banks of the Missouri River. It is estimated that between 1871 and 1884 more than 4 000 Métis migrated west from Manitoba, mainly to Saskatchewan (Sprague, 1988: 139). The federal government initiated a scrip certificate system of land grants whereby the bearers of such certificates, as they were known, could trade for land or cash on presentation of said certificate. Scrip certificates were issued to individual Métis to satisfy their land claim entitlement although the concept first originated in 1873 when they were made available to the original white settlers in Manitoba. After 1885 the certificates were awarded to four categories of recipients; Métis, volunteers who had fought against the Métis, veterans of the Boer War, and officers of the Mounted Police. The scrip certificates given to the Métis after 1885 generated the most controversy, basically because of negative attitudes towards the Métis (Purich, 1988: 107-108).

A look at Riel's life from 1878 to 1884 shows a mixture of searching for and holding various jobs, but always with a concern for his people. On March 6, 1882, a priest blessed his common-law marriage to Marguerite Bellhumeur whose family originated in Quebec and was now domicile with a Cree tribe in the area of Fort Ellis in Montana. Marguerite's father had married a member of the Cree First Nation and settled amongst her people. Riel's wife, Marguerite, bore him two children, a son, Jean, on May 4, 1882, and a daughter, Marie Angelique, on September 17, 1883. There is some indication that Riel neglected his wife because of his travels across the prairies seeking to aid his people in their cause. During his absences, Riel always wrote caring letters to Marguerite affirming his love and concern for her. Riel worked for a while as a schoolteacher for the Jesuits, and although he was dedicated and praised for his work, by 1884, he could not resist the pressure to become publicly involved with the Métis cause.

The Second Campaign

On June 4, 1884, Louis Riel had three visitors from the north, Gabriel Dumont, Michel Dumas, and James Isbister. Trouble was brewing back home and Riel's supporters sought his leadership. During Riel's absence, English and French Métis in Red River had organized a front under the influence of their leader's name and the stage was set for revolt. Riel heard out his visitors' request to join with them, then retreated for the night to deliberate about returning to Manitoba. In the morning his gave his friends his response in writing. He had decided to help the cause, so on June 5, 1884, Riel prepared to take his family north to claim the land he believed rightfully belonged to the Métis (Coates, 1990).

The first shots in the Métis war of 1885 were fired by "Gentleman Joe MacKay" on March 26, 1885, on orders from Major Crozier of the Mounted Police. It was in some ways an unfortunate and unplanned event that served only to further plunge the country into war. The forces of Métis leader, Isidore Dumont, a brother of Gabriel Dumont, sighted Crozier's men near Duck Lake, Saskatchewan, and Dumont and an assistant rode towards Crozier carrying a white flag. When Dumont's assistant reached for his rifle in response to seeing one pointed at him, Crozier gave the order to shoot. Dumont's assistant, a Cree named Assywin, was killed immediately and Dumont was fired upon next. As both men fell dead from their horses, other soldiers started firing. Rifle shots were heard in nearby Batoche where Riel and his men were and they hurried to help their comrades.

Riel's Defeat

One of the reasons for Riel's eventual defeat stemmed from the lack of support for his cause by several disillusioned and sometimes dissident Native minorities. Flanagan (1979a:109) contends that astute chiefs like Sitting Bull, Big Bear, and Crowfoot regarded Riel with suspicion and might have thought that Riel was interested in gaining Aboriginal support merely for his own purposes. Relations between the First Nations and Métis were not necessarily congenial and there was sometimes jealousy between them. From the Métis perspective, Status Indians had reserve lands allotted to them backed by treaties, and they were also the occasional recipients of government rations, while the Métis had neither reserves nor rations (Sealey & Lussier, 1975: 113). A corollary factor was that government spokespersons also tried very hard to discourage Status Indians from cooperating with Riel. In 1879, for example, Crowfoot's followers were instructed by the Indian Commissioner to winter further south so that they would be away from Riel's influence (Flanagan, 1979a: 107). White settlers cared little about the Métis cause and very few of them had much contact with either the Métis or Status Indians in the area.

On March 27, 1885, Major-General Frederick Dobson Middleton arrived in Winnipeg by train and aimed for a quick takeover of the Métis capital of Batoche. Middleton decided that he would take Batoche from the east using Qu'Appelle as a base. The Métis forces barely numbered 300, and Middleton had 5 456 junior officers and 800 soldiers under his command (Charlebois, 1975: 155; Bowsfield, 1971: 125). He also brought 586 horses, eight 9-pounder cannons, various other firearms, and an ample supply of ammunition to the battlefield. The odds were somewhat uneven, since Middleton's officers alone outnumbered the total number of Métis fighting men.

As the battle got underway, Riel's general Gabriel Dumont, who had experience as a military strategist, disagreed with Riel about the best way to engage Middleton's forces. After some discussion he yielded to the wishes of his visionary leader and was severely hampered by Riel's lack of experience in the fighting trenches. Dumont wanted to stage a series of guerrilla-type onslaughts, but Riel's strategy was to hold up in a strong defendable position so that negotiations with government leaders could resume. Had Dumont's plan been executed the war might have gone on for many years as Dumont would have scattered Middleton's troops across the prairies in search of the enemy. Coupled with the fact that the majority of Middleton's troops were almost completely without military experience, the outcome might have been entirely different. As Dumont later stated:

> But my idea is to engage them several times with portions of my force; gradually to fall back, and then fight at my final ground the battle which shall decide who is master in these territories, the half-breeds or the Canadian volunteers. (Anonymous, 1885: 161)

Middleton's military actions have been scrutinized by historians in various ways, some contending that he did not move as quickly as he might have or he could have ended the war much sooner. Middleton was accused of stalling his attack, perhaps because he feared the power and determination of the Métis. Other analysts have come to his rescue by pointing out that the general wanted to make sure of his superior military power before he moved on the enemy (Mulvaney, 1885: 194). Middleton was accused of poor judgment because he divided his troops so they could engage as many of the enemy as they could at once (Hildebrandt, 1989: 109). In any event when the battle was over the record shows that Middleton lost eight men and 46 were wounded; the Métis lost 16 men and 30 were wounded.

Gabriel Dumont Tombstone at Batoche

Descriptions of the various battles fought by the Riel's troops are well documented and need not be elaborated in this context. An admixture of motivations inspired the various battles; for example, some battles were responses to the behavior of government troops who, following orders, burned Métis homes, and destroyed food supplies. On April 2, 1885, the Crees of Frog Lake rose up and killed Indian agents and priests in response to the government's practice of withholding food supplies from hungry people. Fort Pitt, a Hudson's Bay Company post on the Alberta-Saskatchewan border, was also taken (McLean, 1985: 113-116). While these battles were fierce and bloody, the Métis provisional government forbad the killing of civilians. Before enemy engagement, all matters pertaining to war and the survival of the people were discussed and resolved in council.

It is interesting to note that a steamer, the *Northcote,* became the first navel venture of the Canadian military. The steamer was launched on the South Saskatchewan River on April 3, 1885, constructed partly using pieces of Gabriel Dumont's former house and barn for construction. The boat was prepared by Middleton to carry 50 men and serve as a surprise site from which to fire on Batoche from the river. As it turned out the Métis were ready for the steamer's arrival and dropped a cable across the river to block its course. The cable was lowered a little too late but managed to break off two smokestacks, the mast, two tall spars, and the whistle which was flung on the upper deck. The tack was successful, and the poor helmsman tried to steer his course while lying on the ship's floor to avoid being hit by Métis bullets. A crewsman shouted steering orders from a hiding place in another part of the steamer. When the smokestacks were later resurrected, the *Northcote* arrived back at Batoche just in time to blow its whistle for the victory celebration (Howard, 1974: 465).

Site where the *Northcote* was Disabled

A number of historic sites figured in the series of battles ascribed to the Métis war including Frog Lake, Fort Pitt, Fort Carlton, Cutknife, Battleford, Fish Creek, Frenchman's Butte, Duck

Lake, and finally Batoche. At that site, after less than a week of combat, on May 15, 1885, Louis Riel gave himself up to three mounted police scouts and was taken to General Middleton's headquarters. Six days later he entered the barracks of the Mounted Police and when the gates closed behind the Métis leader for the last time, observers thought that they simultaneously closed "...on the hopes and aspirations of the new nation" (Stanley, 1963: 339).

Métis Rifle Pit

An Assessment

As time has passed Louis Riel has become more of a hero to Canadians than he was a century ago. He may have been executed by government authority, but his cause lives on, encouraged no doubt, by his actions and the resultant mythology evolving out of his cause. His death sentence does not stand out as one of the best examples of Canadian "due process," for his captors were too eager to make an example of him. Two decades ago it could be said that the Métis hardly made an impression on the Canadian consciousness (Berger, 1982: 26), but today this is no longer the case. Subsequent happenings including inclusion in constitutional talks during the 1980s have rendered that statement obsolete. Riel may have perished, but a century later his dreams were revitalized. Spurred on by this reality, Riel's followers continue to push for national recognition of their cause and identity.

It is not without some emotion that Riel is hailed as one of the Fathers of Manitoba for he was most certainly involved in formalizing the constitution of Manitoba's first provisional government. The new province was decided upon as the result of a bargain struck with the inhabitants and given legal validity in the *Manitoba Act*, a Canadian law later confirmed by the British Parliament (Lower, 1977: 360). To the Métis, Riel is definitely a hero, but because there are those who oppose this view, he has simultaneously inspired hatred and idolatry, and admiration and contempt (Friesen, 1985: 112). Perhaps as is so often the case, and as time goes on, historians will rewrite the legacy of Riel with a softer pen, and in this way they will catch up with the rising crescendo of Riel's popularity.

The most painful line of evaluation for Riel's life and work was elaborated in his trial when his lawyers defended him on the grounds of insanity. Riel objected to this defence, and protested that he was being made to choose between two equally undesirable options. In his words,

> I would have to defend myself against the accusation of high treason, or I have to consent to an animal life in an asylum. I don't care much about animal life if I am not allowed to carry with it the moral existence of an intellectual being. (Anderson, 1955: 70)

It is unfortunate that Riel's lawyers pled insanity for their client, mainly because of the negativity with which such a plea was viewed at the time. Because of the immense significance that Riel's career has had for western Canada, the shadow hovering over his psychological profile has too long remained and served to affect any objective evaluation of his contributions. Knox (1978) contends that if Riel was psychologically unstable, why were there no references to this before his trial, and why would supposedly sane men follow a mentally unbalanced leader? In the final analysis, does this mean that if a government representative fights hard for the rights of one's constituents, it is necessarily an irrational act?

Batoche Church

The accusation that Louis Riel was bereft of reason, or at least mentally unbalanced, has adequately been commented upon by his biographers. Flanagan (1979b) contends that analysts have neglected to place sufficient emphasis on the influence of religion in Riel's life, implying that Riel's religious philosophy was a major driving force. Much of Riel's earlier life occurred in the context of religious institutions and, as mentioned previously, he was serious enough about his faith to contemplate entering the priesthood. By the mid 1870s he was experiencing considerable guilt over having changed his mind about entering church ministry and worried that he may have missed his calling.

Interior of Batoche Church

Stanley (1963) suggests that Riel gradually developed a mysticism and a sense of self-abasement which must have appeared strange to his former mentors, Archbishop Tache and Abbe Ritchot. When he travelled to Washington in 1874 Riel indicated that a spirit had visited him (the same spirit who had showed himself to Moses in biblical times), and said to Riel, "Rise up, Louis David Riel. You have a mission to perform" (Bowsfield, 1971: 74). Later, on board a train bound for Montreal Riel is reported to have shouted to the passengers at the top of his voice, "I am a prophet!" (Stanley, 1963: 223-224). Shortly thereafter, on March 6, 1876, Riel was admitted as a patient at the Hospital of St. Jean de Dieu at Longue Pointe under the name of Louis R. David. Several months later he was also a patient at an asylum in Beauport near Quebec. On January 28, 1878, he was discharged and certified as cured, but he was warned to avoid excitement (Stanley, 1978). For the next several years, until he visited Manitoba in 1883, he managed to heed that advice. Then, amid appeals to the old days of the provisional government and his patriotism, of ten years earlier, Riel's patriotic juices stirred with excitement. This air of anticipation was heightened a year later when the delegation of his compatriots from Canada came south to lure him back into action.

The information pertaining to Riel's hospitalization period is scant. Naturally, asylums in 1876 did not keep records in the manner that such institutions do today. The occasional official hospital entries related to Riel's stay show that he was admitted with "delusions of grandeur," which today might be interpreted as "depressive mania." On two occasions, March 19 and April 16, 1876, he engaged in acts of destruction and broke furniture in his room. When he left the asylum in 1877, he apparently "showed a slight improvement." Prior to his trial, however, Riel's lawyers searched desperately for evidence of his insanity. They finally came up with two items pertaining to: (i) his confinement in asylums, and (ii) his split with the church and his action towards the clergy. Naturally, the evidence was so weak that the Crown found Riel sane, much to Riel's own delight and that of his captors, who could now legally hang him (Knox, 1978). That event occurred on November 16, 1885.

St. Boniface Cathedral in Winnipeg – Riel Burial Site

Flanagan (1979b) suggests that Riel's religion was a form of millenarianism which absorbed his very being. This interpretation prognosticates an intrigue worth following up and with some analysis may reverse the traditional notion that Riel's religion was merely a symptom of his psychiatric condition. This thesis may also suggest a more objective foundation upon which to evaluate the man and his work.

There are ample references to religious concepts and processes in Riel's letters and other writings and Riel's biographers includes many such examples in outlining the various stages of his life. It is argued that Riel believed during the course of this life that he was endowed by God with a special mission as a "Prophet of the New World." He was to be responsible for ushering in a new Kingdom of God for the Métis people that would assure them of a land-based future. During the campaign of the 1880s this conviction became the major controlling force of his mind (Flanagan, 1979b, vii). Riel was known to have quoted King David on occasion, claiming in reference to his enemies that he, Riel, would ". . . beat them as small as the dust of the earth: I shall crush them and spread them abroad like the mire of the streets" (Howard, 1974: 321).

Braz (2003: 3) is probably accurate when he suggests that the reason why perceptions of Riel's role in Canadian history is so fraught with controversy is because assessments of his life and times are more than anything else reflective of the social realities in which the writers lived. Too often analysts steep their evaluations of Riel's work in EuroCanadian contexts rather than in Métis contexts. The result is that Riel is criticized from within a frame of reference that does not fit. When Métis writers undertake this task, they naturally embellish Riel's contributions partially in an effort to make up for undue criticisms his campaign has received. If Braz is right, future literature about the Métis and Louis Riel should show more of a balance between the polemic of the past and the antithetical efforts of Riel's admirers.

Louis Riel is clearly not the only historical figure who made claims about being Divinely-connected. The similarities of behavior exhibited by him and other inspired leaders are in many ways overwhelming. One key difference appears to be that Riel was executed for his actions by his own countrymen. In the final analysis, however, even that act backfired because Riel's execution served his cause well. Even now, more than a century later, his cause lives on in the visions and actions of his people.

Martin Heath is not the only one to believe in Riel's mission, but he has poetically described Riel's heroism this way;

In our early western story, Riel fought to have men free,

Shared his heart with white and Métis, in the cause of democracy. His the voice of the Red River, His the spirit of our folk,

When they banded all together, to defeat a tyrant's yoke (Braz, 2003: 103).

Visitor Reception – Batoche Historical Park

Church Cemetery at Batoche

5
Images

When you want to understand Squatterville, you begin to understand some crucial aspects of the life of native people and Métis in Canada. – writer Heather Robertson. (August, 1970: 17)

If the Métis people are going to remain culturally distinctive, they must resist assimilation. Such resistance cannot be taken for granted, for without conscious effort, this is the most probable outcome. – Lance Roberts, Susanne von Below, and Mathias Bos. (2001: 195)

Little changed in regard to Métis culture and identity after Riel's defeat in 1885 and assimilation into the mainstream was both a societal impossibility and an undesirable state of affairs from the Métis perspective. For a long time after Riel's departure the federal government insisted that its obligations to the Métis ended after Ottawa dealt with their land claims under the *Manitoba Act*. The official stance was that the matter had been dealt with by arranging for land allowances in the Territories in 1885 and 1899-1900 (Francis, Jones and Smith, 1988: 337).

After the Battle of Batoche the Métis were quite simply an unwanted people who despaired of the inevitability of melting into mainstream society represented by the incoming Europeans. In fact, the two Native-derived cultures of Métis and "English half-breeds" (Spry, 2001: 109) existed side by side in Red River, albeit virtually independently, for fifty years before the transfer of the territory to Canada. The two groups comprised quite distinct societies in major ways; the Métis were French-speaking and Roman Catholic by faith, and the English-speaking mixed-bloods were Protestants. The two communities occupied neighboring parishes, occasionally intermarried, and sometimes cooperated on political causes (Mailhot and Sprague, 1985: 1-2).

Sprague (1988: 184) contends that the Riel "Rebellion" itself was not the result of cultural misunderstanding, but simply a story of government manipulation of the Manitoba Métis since 1869. McLean (1985: 123) goes further and suggests that the Canadian federal government was actively involved with local party investors and speculators in an effort to create a Métis resistance. The government hoped that a civil war would create an atmosphere to protect economic monopolies, such as the Canadian Pacific Railway, in order to exploit the west. Even the church fathers to whom the Métis had always been faithful, united their voices with those of the Orangemen to keep the Canadians from showing mercy to Riel's people (de Tremaudan, 1982: 195). Thus, after 1885 the Métis remained a culturally unique people although they did not have the dignity of recognition as a legally-separate people which the treaties granted to Status Indians (Woodcock, 1976: 249).

Social conditions forced some Métis to seek adoption into First Nations communities by virtue of their Indian ancestry. A few families negotiated their way to legal status while others fled to the northern region of Saskatchewan to the Prince Albert area, and to Peace River country in Alberta. A third faction of Métis decided to redeem the scrip certificates which the government made available to them. These could be exchanged for either money or land in selected areas (Stanley, 1960: 378). Many Métis quickly disposed of the scrip certificates for cash, sometimes at ridiculously low prices, and tried to compete with members of dominant society as farmers, small merchants, or artisans. Their shanty-like homes were often built at the edge of settlements or on road allowances scattered throughout the area (Adams, 1975).

Scrip

The legal basis of Métis scrip is the *Manitoba Act* of 1870, which was brought into effect at the time of the first provincial election held that year. Although the *Manitoba Act* was the first piece of legislation in Canada specifically to recognize the Aboriginal rights of the halfbreeds, as the Métis were called, it made no mention of scrip. The Act merely stated the amount of land to be awarded and specified that the grant was to be for the benefit of "children of the Half-Breed heads of families." A later amendment in 1874, extended recognition to the halfbreed heads of families who had been excluded from the *Manitoba Act,* and explicitly stated that compensation was to be made to them as well. Still later, an Order-in-Council specifically spelled out that no other means of compensation, only scrip should be issued to satisfy the claims under the Act of 1870 (Métis Association of Alberta, 1981: 92).

Ironically, in the case of white settlers who were also granted scrip privileges, there was a unanimous decision in parliament to grant scrip to both adults and children alike. This inequitable action was taken a scant two weeks after Métis children were awarded their rights. Métis halfbreed parents had to wait an inordinate length of time before they were awarded scrip (Métis Association of Alberta, 1981: 104).

The foundational plank for designing scrip was to reward the Métis and European settlers for their efforts in bringing the country into civilization, and help them in reestablishing themselves in regions other than the Red River area. Basically a scrip document was a certificate which entitled the bearer to receive land or money and could be redeemed whenever the bearer was ready to do so. In certain scrip issues in Manitoba, however, some halfbreed families were specifically given money scrip which could not be redeemed for land (Métis Association of Alberta, 1981: 106).

Both Métis and nonNative recipients of scrip certificates equally favored the idea of scrip since by jointly supporting it they assured themselves of a future land base (Flanagan, 1991a: 135). A resolution was adopted to assure that all original settlers would be participants in the plan, not just those identified by Lord Selkirk. Land was evaluated at one dollar per acre and adult recipients were awarded batches of eight scrips worth $20.00 each for an intended total of 160 acres of land. Children were to receive 240 acres or $240.00 worth of scrip. By April 7, 1885, a commission authorized to hand out scrip certificates arrived in local communities. A total of 3 186 scrips were designated for Métis and 800 for original white settlers. Métis lands were to total 1 400 000 acres (566 801 hectares) but it was specified that they were specifically targeted for the halfbreed children who were resident in the province at the time of the transfer of the territory.

Scrip certificate distribution went on for many years. Purich (1988: 111) estimates that from 1885 to 1921, twelve Half-Breed Commissions travelled throughout the northwestwest to enumerate Métis and issue scrip. The last certificate was dated April 3, 1907. It is difficult to pinpoint who actually claimed scrip certificates, although signing for them was the mandated practice. A power of attorney was allegedly often initiated so that original claimants cannot be identified. Government distributers did not always try to validate the re-assignment of the scrip; they were only charged with making the certificates available. As a result, only a small list of signatures applying for scrip has been located (Flanagan, 1991a: 140-141).

The controversy emanating from the issue of scrip has to do with possible fraud committed against the Métis over the years. Sealey and Lussier (1975) contend that those Métis who stayed around to collect scrip actually received little financial benefit. These recipients soon discovered that the money value of scrip could only produce half its face value so they sold the scrip hastily and spent the money, possibly buying merchandise or services of no utility. The resultant short-lived income only aided them in developing further negative attitudes towards white society and contributed towards their own misery and discouragement (Giraud, 1956; Stanley, 1960; Friesen, 1987).

Flanagan (1983) has perhaps been the strongest proponent of the idea that the Métis were well compensated after the Riel civil war in 1885. He argues that after victory was declared by government forces, the Métis were financially destitute and needed cash; they saw selling scrip as a quick way to get it. According to Flanagan the Métis were skilled traders and often bargained intently with purchasers of their scrips. There was also competition among buyers which appeared to work in favor of the Métis (Purich, 1988: 118). Giraud (1956) contends that the Métis eagerly sold their scrip for a sum of money lower than its value because they needed cash. A title worth $240 was generally bought up for $165, while one worth $160 would go for $110. With the money in hand the Métis sellers found it easier to flee from Manitoba and seek refuge further west (Sprague, 1991).

Hicks and Morgan (2001: 176) seem to agree with this interpretation, pointing out that scrip offered a preferable alternative for those Métis who wished to relocate and continue an independent economic existence. Scrip could be sold and the recipients of money could undertake a fresh start and pursue an independent lifestyle. Ens (1988) disputes this interpretation, arguing that the Dominion land surveyors recognized the validity of Métis occupancy, or those to whom they had sold these rights, and difficulties encountered in obtaining title did not play an important part in encouraging Métis emigration from Manitoba (Ens, 1988; Flanagan, 1991b).

The shadier side of the scrip story has to do with the fact that large quantities of scrip certificates fell into the hands of land speculators who anticipated high land prices. Wise speculators inspected the lands before buying the certificates, often choosing locations near to possible railway routes. Later, groups of speculators formed land companies and connected with agents who brought settlers west to purchase and occupy such lands. Evidently huge profits could materialize through careful planning (Lussier and Sealey, 1978: 40). The Métis Association of Alberta (1981: 110) contends that most of the rules, regulations and legislative acts pertaining to scrip appear to have been designed to get scrip out of Métis hands as fast as possible.

Purich's discussion is helpful here. He refers to the work of the Gabriel Dumont Institute in Regina which investigated the phenomenon of scrip and found, for example, that a random search of the names of persons who redeemed scrip revealed 1 886 people with surnames starting with the letters L through Z. Of these, 346 certificates were issued to people whose surnames began with the letters, L and M. Further, it was found that 33 of the 346 certificates were owned by one company, Osler and Hammond of Toronto. The Merchants Bank of Winnipeg acquired 38, and two Winnipeg bankers personally held 23 certificates. In light of this evidence, Purich contends that there was indeed fraud regarding scrip and raises the question, "Did the government know about the fraud?" His own position is, "There can . . . be no question that outright fraud was committed against the Métis. All that remains unknown is the extent of the fraud" (Purich, 1988: 25).

Restructuring Lifestyle

The response of Manitoba Canadians to the Métis people after 1885 was void of sympathy for their cause. Initially European newcomers to the west resolved to prove their loyalty to eastern Canada by isolating themselves from any Métis interests. They therefore applauded the defeat of the Métis and found themselves polarized in demanding the death of Louis Riel. Métis resistance had threatened to impede further settlement in the west, possibly reducing potential economic expansion. Now, with the war over, it could be business as usual. Coates (1990) observes that this did not turn out to be the case. In fact, after Riel's imprisonment, western Manitobans forgot their earlier platitudes about national unity and the new sense of purpose derived from the battle against a common enemy. To some extent the old east versus west battle lines re-emerged, and those new settlers who migrated to the west carried with them negative perceptions of First Nations and Métis. They described the Aboriginal peoples as dirty, diseased, and demoralized, and viewed them as impediments to civilized development. According to their perceptions, it would be difficult to build a new society as long as the Métis were around.

The record shows that immigration to Canada was severely curtailed by the news of the Riel war. In 1885 the number of immigrants who migrated to Canada declined to 79 160 that year from a high of 133 624 in 1883 and 103 824 in 1884. Obviously the area most affected was the west, basically because of antagonistic publicity surrounding the civil war. Only 21 946 individuals migrated to Manitoba and the Territories in 1885, and of that total, 14 706 were reported to have left the prairies for the United States, leaving only 7 240 immigrants in 1885 (Lalonde, 1974). Some of the settlers who remained actually benefited from the war and procured jobs as guides, teamsters, linemen, and messengers. Those who chose agriculture as a lifestyle, and were successful at it, sold their goods at a high market value.

While many Métis in Manitoba departed for points west and south (Montana and Dakota Territory), after 1885, those who remained faced an uphill struggle to rebuild their lifestyle. Those groups who refused to work the land had an especially difficult time and many relied on charity for long periods of time before a permanent source of income could be established. Some heads of families cut wood or harvested hay while others were employed in gathering buffalo bones that had accumulated in their hunting grounds over the years previous and were now manufactured into fertilizer. Some Métis sought to assimilate into the larger society and migrated to the towns to fit in; others simply gave in to discouragement and poverty and lived a day-to-day existence. This condition enhanced the motivation of religious missionaries who attempted to turn things around for the Métis by initiating limited social reforms and by preaching against drunkenness and moral degradation. They also urged the Métis to occupy new lands further west and tried to shift their values to an agrarian lifestyle.

St. Paul des Métis Colony

In 1895, the spectacle of the debilitating conditions and growing misery among the Métis inspired two priests, Father Joseph-Adeodat Therien and Father Albert Lacombe, to do something about it. They proposed that the federal government establish a series of Métis reserves that would assure them of a land-space and comprise a specific means for them to upgrade their standard of living and to perpetuate their culture. The proposed plan was entitled, "A Philanthropic Plan to Redeem the Half-Breeds of Manitoba and the Territories," and was shown to be feasible in light of past mishandled scrip dealings and other political foibles.

On December 28, 1895, a federal Order-in-Council was passed which established the first such colony. The St. Paul des Métis colony came into being near the Saddle Lake Indian Reserve in Alberta, on a 21 year lease, on Townships 57 and 58, Ranges 9 and 10, east of the Fourth Meridian. The leases were to be $1.00 per year and a board of management was to be formed by members of the Oblate Order.

Father Albert Lacombe envisaged that an agricultural theme would be central to the St. Paul Colony, and the government worked with the priests in offering land, equipment, livestock, and schools as means by which to help the Métis adjust to life in the west. Specifically, the Métis were promised the construction of a technical school, a church, an allocation of livestock, and an 80 acre piece of land for each family. As Father Lacombe told the Métis;

> In a short time you will have made an establishment which will afford you an easy living and you will have the consolation to be at home, near your church, your school, and your pastors. (Métis Association of Alberta, 1981: 167)

When the colony opened its first year in 1896 it was too late to plant crops so the residents supported themselves by winter fishing. The next year a crop was sown, and a sawmill and a gristmill were moved from Lac La Biche and reconstructed on the property. The Oblates encouraged the development of hogfarms and other related industries, but spent most of their time in educational and religious teaching and administration. A few years later, when Clifford Sifton was replaced as Minister of the Interior by Frank Oliver, the benefits of a brief government patronage relationship seem to have helped the colony. Under Oliver's leadership the government picked up some bills which the colony incurred, perhaps as a goodwill gesture on the part of the new administration (Métis Association of Alberta, 1981: 171).

The St. Paul Colony operated only for a few years and then its operation ceased. This happening was explained differently by various sources including government, the church, and Métis occupants. The Métis Association of Alberta reports that the colony had a very hard time, largely because the government had little confidence in the "redemption of the Métis" and scuttled the venture by holding back on necessary funding. Ecclesiastical justification for the colony's failure was furnished by Emeric O. Drouin, OMI (1963), who suggested that many of the efforts initiated at the colony did bear fruit. The second epoch, 1901 to 1905, in fact, witnessed material and spiritual progress, so that hopes of attaining the proposed goal became firmly rooted. Acknowledging the lack of financial backing and the absence of proper instructors, Drouin also blamed the Métis themselves for the colony's failure because "the Métis, lacking so much in ambition and energy, had to be given the example of experienced farmers around them" (Drouin, 1963: 13-14). Naturally, those who lived on the colony and worked its various sectors, strongly disagreed with these explanations.

The St. Paul project started out with three families in 1895 and 30 more families joined almost immediately thereafter in response to Father Lacombe's call. Lands were allotted, but residents soon complained that they had no livestock or agricultural equipment.

By 1897, 50 families had arrived, a school was started, and the community struggled on. It turned out that the principle obstacle was the continual plea for operating capital coupled with the reality that the farmland could barely supply enough food for the assembled population (Giraud, 1956). By 1905, however, the handwriting was on the wall. To begin with, that year the residential school burned down and there was no money to rebuild it. In addition, Father Therien encouraged the government to open up settlement lands around the colony in hopes of attracting French-Canadians to move there. According to the Métis Association of Alberta, he also encouraged the Métis to leave the colony because he was dissatisfied with their progress and hoped to replace them with French-Canadian immigrants.

By 1908 the project was officially abandoned and settlement lands were thrown open to non-Métis settlers. According to one source, the priests urged French Canadians to move to the community, hoping that their energies would encourage the Métis to try harder, but the result was that the Métis moved away (Palmer and Palmer, 1990: 102). The Métis Association of Alberta argues that this was a replacement, not a supplemental manoeuvre. The organization contends that Father Therien himself notified French-Canadian settlers of the date that the colony lands would be opened and warned them to stand in line at the Edmonton Land Office to register. Apparently 250 French-Canadians registered the first day (Métis Association of Alberta, 1981: 178). Thus, after several decades of struggle to carve out a satisfactory lifestyle with a good future for their children, the population dwindled as one by one the Métis families opted for fresh starts elsewhere. Giraud (1956) notes that the failure of Lacombe's experiment left the Métis a prey to suspicion and fostered resentment against the missionaries who were accused of primarily serving the interests of French-Canadians. Drouin (1963) defends the church's record at St. Paul through the efforts of Father Therien who failed at this colony but later redeemed himself through similar efforts at Lafond, St. Edouard, St. Vincent, and Bonnyville. Métis leaders today contend that the failure of the experiment was indicative of the odds that were stacked against their people which almost certainly dictated a bleak future for them. They argue that the decade of the 1890s marked the beginning of an economic slump in which most Métis still find themselves today (Métis Association of Alberta, 1981: 161). Generally-speaking, the Métis in Canada today still face appalling social conditions and higher than average rates of poverty and incarceration (Dorion and Préfontaine, 2001: 34). Most Canadians are probably not even aware of this deplorable situation. In an effort to gain public attention, Métis leaders are stepping up their involvement in the political arena.

Métis Colonies

Because of the inadequacy of the scrip program, it became evident in the 1930s that many Métis did not hold property title to lands which they occupied. In many cases they were legally considered squatters. The first step to alleviate this situation occurred in Alberta in 1929 when a small band of Métis in the Cold Lake area of Alberta grouped together to petition the government for land ownership. Some of the petitioners were former St. Paul occupants, and because of their past experiences they realized the value of more permanent holdings. In 1932 the organization they formed became known as The Métis Association of Alberta with Joe Dion as its first president. The organization grew rapidly and soon identified eleven potential sites for Métis communities. The provincial government responded to their petitions in February, 1933, by authorizing an investigation into the quality of Métis life in the province. Two years later the Ewing Commission was appointed to enquire into the health, education, and general welfare of the half-breed population of the province.

The Ewing Commission reported on February 15, 1936, emphasizing that a band-aid solution for the Métis problem (the word halfbreed was visibly omitted in their report), would be impracticable. Indeed a long-term solution was needed. The commission recognized that the Métis must take up farming, and recommended that a small agricultural community experiment be initiated as a model for others to follow. The commission also stressed that the Métis should be afforded a measure of independence in developing such a community.

In 1938, it was announced by the Government of Alberta through the *Métis Population Betterment Act* that 70 townships of land would be set aside to develop a series of permanent Métis settlements or "colonies" as they were also called. The total number of acres allotted would be determined by the number of families applying. The final calculation showed that 320 acres per family were to be awarded. The Métis occupying these colonies would not be considered wards of the state and they would not be required to pay lease fees for the land. Three-man advisory boards would constitute governing authorities for the colonies and they would have authority to ban non-Métis from the colonies, hire their own schoolteachers, and operate colony schools (Dobbin, 1981: 117-118). The term, "Métis" was re-defined as a person with not less than one-quarter Indian blood but who was neither a Status Indian nor a nonStatus Indian according to the Indian Act. A series of amendments followed the Act, each clarifying some aspect of the overall plan in accordance with the philosophy of trying to be flexible to the needs of the Métis people (Métis Association of Alberta, 1981).

The Métis colonies were born out of the common misery and poverty of the Great Depression which was particulary hard on the Métis. The colonies were supposed to represent a provincial response to the existence of federal Indian reserves, but, as Chalmers (1967: 268) notes, they were more nearly an echo. The people who settled on them found themselves in a paternalistic bureaucracy which made all of the decisions affecting the colonies. The Métis did not obtain actual title to colony lands; thus they were actually only tenants with no rights of authority. This meant that they had no decision-making powers so that they could not forbid nonMétis from moving onto the colonies, determine who would teach their children, or govern how their schools would be operated. In effect, when it came to major decisions, every move the residents made had to be approved by outside authorities.

By the 1940s the colonies took shape. The Métis were given relief in return for building roads into the colonies, preparing village sites, and cutting timber to build their homes and schools. Dramatic differences among the colonies arose. The more successful ones were in the Peace River area including Keg River (Paddle Prairie), Big Prairie, High Prairie, and Utikuma Lake (also known as Atikameg Colony), and relied heavily on commercial fishing and provincial highway construction. The colonies in the north-eastern part of the province included Elizabeth, Fishing Lake, Wolf Lake, and Goodfish, but did not fare as well because jobs were scarce and the rewards of hunting and fishing were minimal. Because of this situation three sites originally set aside for additional colonies were withdrawn at Métis' request as unsuitable (Dobbin, 1981: 130). By 1943 many residents of the northeast colonies migrated to the Keg River Colony (Paddle Prairie) and readjusted their lifestyle to an agricultural base.

A special concern on the Métis colonies was the quality of education available to children of colony residents. As early as the 1950s some Métis children in northern regions also attended public school systems. In Alberta, for example, they were enrolled in the High Prairie School Division, the Athabasca Division, or the Lac La Biche Division. Generally speaking, the quality of education on the colonies was very poor since facilities were minimal and teachers ill-qualified. Some children were admitted to federal Indian schools as guests although they were quickly turned away if space was limited. Since not all of the children in the north could be accommodated by the means available, by 1960 a number of independent school districts were established in the north.

In Saskatchewan a model for northern schooling had been developed that intrigued educators across the west. A departmental officer was appointed to look after northern school services under a centralized administration located in Prince Albert. Alberta and Manitoba leaders followed this example and soon developed independent school districts for these purposes. In 1960, Alberta developed the Northland School Division and thus became the first province to recognize the unique cultural situation of the north and modify its system accordingly (Chalmers, 1967: 270-272). The story of the Northland School Division is described in the next chapter.

Saskatchewan Inaction

The Saskatchewan chapter on Métis colonies began in 1944 when the CCF party came to power under the leadership of Premier T. C. Douglas. Only a few colonies were slated for development and they never progressed past the experimental stage. The word "colony" was actually used in connection with one site only, the government preferring the term "rehabilitation settlements." Designed for the southern part of the province where the most disadvantaged groups of Métis lived, the socialist policies of the Douglas government dictated that they do something for the Métis. Another motivating factor was the extent of racism practiced against the Saskatchewan Métis; their children were not wanted in public schools, and Métis communities generally were targets of overt acts of prejudice and discrimination (Barron, 1990). The anticipated governmental design for the Saskatchewan colonies was to form an agrarian base even though many of the residents preferred to work for wages. Much of the land selected for the colonies was poor in quality and the Saskatchewan government was new and inexperienced in the business of industrial development. Their policies reflected the social philosophy of the time and government leaders basically made plans for the Métis without too much consultation. In this they followed the procedures of the federal government in dealing with Status Aboriginals.

National Focus

The 1960s witnessed the birth and growth of a number of national Métis organizations such as the Manitoba Métis Federation, the Ontario Métis and Non-Status Indian Association, and the Louis Riel Métis Association of British Columbia. The Métis Nation of Ontario was formed in 1994, after a founding delegates meeting that included Métis from across the province.

From 1971 onwards the Native Council of Canada (now the Congress of Aboriginal Peoples (CAP) alone represented Métis interests at the national level. Responsibility for Métis interests was specifically assumed by the Métis National Council (MNC) in 1983 with the mandate to restore Métis lands and resources for future generations and achieve full recognition of the Métis Nation and its jurisdiction within the Canadian federal system. The MNC has been recognized by the United Nations and been granted NonGovernmental Organization status within that organization.

The internal diversity of interests among the Métis has kept them from achieving a strong national voice, partly because the various organizations foster different definitions of who might be accepted as Métis. As Foster (2001: 79) notes,

At this point, the question is of such complexity that just the existence of a "Euro-Canadian" father and an Indian mother no longer constitutes sufficient explanation for Métis origins.

The western Métis still view themselves, as they did a century ago, as a distinct Indigenous nation with a history, culture, and homeland in western Canada and they are generally affiliated with the Métis National Council. Those who define their claims based more on Aboriginal origins rather than national rights appear more inclined (as Métis or nonStatus Indians), to join the Congress of Aboriginal Peoples (Brown, 1987: 144).

In 1969 the Métis Association of Alberta proposed to the provincial Human Resources Development Authority that the Métis situation be re-examined to assess the success of the initial concept of Métis settlements. In 1972 the Task Force identified a serious economic situation in the settlements due to a shortage of investment capital, and recommended that a form of local self-government be established so that the challenge of economic development could be undertaken by the people themselves. The Task Force startled Métis residents by suggesting that the boundaries of the settlements be removed so they could ultimately become part of the general provincial community.

In 1973 the eight Métis settlement associations formed the Alberta Federation of Métis Settlement Associations for the purpose of fighting for land security and local legislative authority, and in order to obtain a sound financial base along their own ideas. The residents wanted to wrest administrative control from the provincial Métis Development Branch. This was an innovative movement towards self-government among Native people and no doubt inspired other Native organizations and communities to adopt a similar course. By 1982 negotiations were underway with the provincial government to achieve additional constitutional protection and, ultimately, to achieve self-government. The move toward self-government occurred against a backdrop of an underlying philosophy of self-determination on the part of provincial Native populations generally, and reflected an enhanced agitation motivated by individuals with a better education, a move to and participation in an urban way of life, and more experience in the political sector. By June 1989, the residents of Alberta's eight Métis settlements approved a government agreement giving the Métis a measure of self-government and 310 million dollars in land compensation which was to be used for economic development (Palmer and Palmer, 1990: 366).

New Hope through Politicization

The Métis struggle for enhanced legal recognition has only very recently reached a measure of fruition. Unlike Status First Nations, the Métis did not have certain entitlements and restrictions that apply to Status Indians. In effect, the differences between Status and nonStatus Indians were mainly based on legal and bureaucratic considerations that had little to do with the cultural attributes of the people (Li, 1988: 23-24). With some exceptions the presence of the Métis has slipped into the annals of the Canadian historical record almost inadvertently. They were listed separately as a people by the Canadian census in 1941 and again in 1981, but the Dominion Bureau of Statistics has consistently failed to cite separate population statistics such as births, marriages, or deaths for them in the Territories (Friesen, 1985: 108). The 1981 Canadian census reported that there were people in every province who call themselves Métis, but their historical origins varied (Peters, Rosenberg and Halseth, 1991: 71). Traditionally, in government record-keeping the Métis were included in other categories, such as "Native Indians, Eskimos, White," etc. As an official once explained it, "It depends on their residence, for example, Indian reserve, urban area, rural or a bush community that is predominantly Eskimo or Indian" (Slobodin, 1966: 9).

The right forcefully to voice their concerns at any meaningful political level for the Métis occurred in January, 1981, when the federal government announced that the proposed Canadian Constitution would recognize and affirm the Aboriginal and Treaty rights of the Indian, Inuit and Métis peoples. It was a major victory, but still a long way from being recognized as the "cornerstone of Canadian Confederation" long espoused by some Métis leaders (Daniels, 1979: 7). That same year, however, the government temporarily dropped the idea of incorporating Aboriginal rights in the Canadian Constitution, claiming that the unanimous consent of the provinces would not be possible if that clause were included. Still later the clause was again picked up with the addition of the word "existing" pertaining to Aboriginal rights. Peter Lougheed, then Premier of Alberta, was the last hold-out and it was he who insisted on the rephrasing of the concept to "existing rights" (Purich, 1988: 169-172).

It is not clear how Métis concerns were included in constitutional talks and several parties claim to have successfully promoted the idea. Some credit the former Native Council of Canada with this recognition, citing it as the most significant achievement of the Council (Gaffney, Gould, and Semple: 1984, 4). The NCC was successful with this adoption even though the government at that time rejected the NCC's land proposals (Weaver, 1985: 97). The Métis combatted criticisms that they did not really constitute an Aboriginal society since they were not even in existence before Indian-white contact. They eagerly trotted out legal documentation to indicate that they were recognized as a distinct people at least since the *Manitoba Act* of 1870 which made specifically mention of them. Documents issuing scrip made numerous references to the Métis people and this fact was used to round out the Métis argument that their identity and history was well established in the nations archives.

The fact that the *Canadian Charter of Rights and Freedoms* of 1982 lists the Métis with Indian and Inuit peoples as "Aboriginal peoples of Canada" may have determined the direction of the supreme court's decision (Driedger, 1989: 381). Constitutional proceedings through 1992 did include mention of the Métis as Aboriginal peoples. It is worth noting that the Supreme Court of Canada dealt with the issue of Métis Aboriginal rights in 1986, but only in relation to the effect an Aboriginal title cession had on federal and provincial jurisdictions. The adjoining discussion was unfortunately superficial in that the court was reluctant to make a decision on the matter except to refer to the Royal Proclamation of 1763 (Gaffney, Gould and Semple, 1984: 100-101). The background to that event has contemporary implications.

When the governing of Canada began under British rule, officials wanted to enlist the help of the First Nations as allies against the French. Two proclamations were issued in this regard, the first by the Privy Council in Great Britain in 1791, which forbad the various colonies from passing any grants on lands owned by the

Indians. The second was the Royal Proclamation of 1763 signed by King George III (Scott-Brown, 1991). The latter was a policy to protect Indian lands even though many British leaders would have thought that signing treaties with the Indians provided this protection (Johnston, 1989). The Royal Proclamation outlined the boundaries for Upper Canada and tried to clarify the pre-existing and conceded rights (including land rights) for the First Nations. The Proclamation did not deal with Indian lands in the west, of course, although English law (which applied to the colonies), stated that citizens of a newly acquired dominion do not lose their property or civil rights (Asch, 1984). These rights were to remain unless the sovereign passed a law which directly diminished the rights of the original inhabitants. The only legislation in Canada that would have done that would be the treaties by which the Indians gave up certain lands and were given compensation for them. Consequently, those Aboriginal peoples who did not sign treaties did not give up their land rights (Scott-Brown, 1991: 100). With the legal recognition of the Métis as Aboriginal peoples it would seem that reference to the Royal Proclamation by the Supreme Court of Canada in 1986 did little to enhance any case against the Métis. This has now been rectified by the supreme court.

The Congress of Aboriginal Peoples, which was founded to represent the interests of Métis and Status Aboriginals who live off-reserve, and the Métis National Council, continue to press on for self-government for Métis people. Their powers and successes will be directly related by the sense of community attained and fostered by members of the Métis community itself. Clearly the Métis, along with Canada's other Native people, are gaining attention as integral players in the nation's past, present, and future. Neither scholars, government, media, nor the Métis themselves are likely to allow this trend to be reversed in the foreseeable future (Brown, 1988: 145).

6

Inculcation

In the past, most curricula and textbooks failed to address the contributions and participation of First Nations and Métis peoples in Canadian society. . . . educational publishing about the Métis is still in its infancy and there is a great need for Métis resources that complement existing curriculum. – Dorion and Préfontaine (2001: 31-32)

To a great extent education will be the key that allows Métis people to enter the mainstream of society and operate within it as equals. The Métis, as a group, have chosen complete integration despite the difficulty in achieving it. Their official organization recognizes progress in education as the factor most likely to assist in achieving that objective. – D. Bruce Sealey and Antoine Lussier (1975: 179)

It seems somewhat ironic that while books about Métis history and culture are proliferating, the educational need identified by Sealey and Lussier in the above quote, is woefully lacking. Instead, both Métis and nonMétis writers have concentrated on historical, political and cultural themes, and neglected the fact that without proper instruction, direct or indirect, no culture can be perpetuated. Writing about Louis Riel and his vision or current Métis political designs may be exhilarating and controversial, but it will not assist the Métis in attaining the measure of nationhood which Riel envisaged for them.

The Manitoba Métis Federation has promoted the concept that economic success and psychological well-being for Métis people will best be accomplished through improved education. Unexamined, however, the fact is that without a clear alternative plan in mind, assimilation is inevitable. Those Métis organizations whose officials subscribe to the Sealey and Lussier thesis, would do well to encourage the formulation of educational resources that would mitigate against the inevitable destiny of their people. As it is, newer generations of Métis are continually reassessing the objectives of the educational milieu in which they are being cast. The happy end result of Métis efforts, will hopefully, comprise a reconciliation of the longstanding federal education policy of assimilation with the campaign for self-determination fostered by most Native communities today (Tobias, 1988: 154, Brookes, 1991).

Many provincial ministries of education are in the process of originating Native Education Branches in order to develop Native studies curricula, evaluate resources, and conduct research on Native educational policies and perspectives. Saskatchewan and Manitoba lead the way in including Aboriginal emphases in school curricula and other provinces are following their lead aided by such organizations as the Gabriel Dumont Institute of Métis Studies and Applied Research, and the Louis Riel Institute of the Manitoba Métis Federation. If they are to be effective, however, these efforts must be supported by the greater Métis community.

Historical Survey

After 1885, things went downhill for Riel's followers. The first half of the twentieth century did not belong to the Métis. Unlike Treaty Indians they did not have legal status nor designated lands to occupy. Of course the establishment of reserves did little to advance First Nations development per se since the Indigenous people were still dependent upon government for subsistence. In the eyes of the Métis, however, Status First Nations at least had a land base.

The educational history of the Métis at the turn of the last century correlated with the span of their economic involvements. After the defeat of Louis Riel in 1885, the Métis basically gravitated toward one of three routes. First, there were those who opted for the more traditional Native way of life whose communities became targets of missionary education. Many bands were receptive to Métis inclusion and thus enlarged their communities to accommodate them. Métis children were thus educated in Indian day schools and later in residential schools.

A second group of Métis migrated west of Manitoba and engaged in various limited or seasonal job markets. Their children got potluck by way of education. Third, there were those who tried to integrate into the society of the incoming Europeans and so were educated in Canada's slowly developing school system.

The educational attainments of the Métis who joined with Aboriginal tribes were dependent upon developments on the Indian reserves. When there was room in reserve schools, Métis children who lived in nearby communities were allowed to attend. Although their parents were not permitted by law to live on the reserve, they basically adopted a reserve type of life. Because of this the Métis needed the same services in education, health, and welfare as Status Indians, but they were not served in this respect by the Indian Affairs Branch of the federal government. Since the provinces were slow to respond to nonStatus needs this segment of Métis fared even worse than their Indian counterparts (Sealey and Lussier, 1975: 147).

The contingent of Métis who opted for life further west after the Riel defeat often found themselves occupying quickly-constructed shantytowns located at the edge of EuroCanadian settlements, however, these communities quickly deteriorated into Canada's first twentieth century slums. The odds were against them, and in the words of Maria Campbell, "So began a miserable life of poverty which held no hope for the future. That generation of my people was completely beaten" (Campbell, 1973: 13).

Western Canadian Métis settlements were unusually stable in nature, unlike the nearby towns where they were situated. The vocations they pursued included agriculture and fishing, and many of the men worked for the railway or in lumber camps or sawmills. Schools in the settlements were mainly established by church denominations, but a lack of funds allowed most of the schools to operate only a few months each year. Thus each succeeding generation of Métis tended to have less schooling than the previous (Sealey, 1980: 38). Many of the Métis settlements endured well past the midpoint of the twentieth century probably basing their durability upon hard work and a variety of secondary factors.

The Métis who adapted most successfully, from an economic point of view, were those who opted for integration into the dominant EuroCanadian culture. Most of them gave up or denied their Aboriginal roots and strove to be accepted by and successful at jobs approved by the Canadian majority (Giraud, 1956). The late Howard Adams, a Native activist and for many years a professor at the University of Saskatchewan, admitted that his own academic and social successes came at the expense of abandoning his Native ancestry and connections. Suddenly, in 1948, when his 52-year-old mother died, he realized that what he had perceived as a cultural albatross really constituted the essence of his very being. (Adams, 1975: 41-43). Was all the denial worth it? According to Adams it was "not–not" with the continual reminder that he had knowingly abandoned his heritage.

Evidently the assimilation process was very effective with the Métis people. According to the 1941 census there were only 26 660 Métis in all of Canada. There were 8 692 Métis in Manitoba, 8 808 in Alberta, and 9 160 in Saskatchewan (Sealey and Lussier, 1975: 140). This compares, for example, with an earlier figure of 10 398 resident Métis in Manitoba in 1870 (Lusty, 1973: 10).

It would be incorrect to suggest that the deplorable educational conditions among northern Métis were always ignored by government. At first the federal government accepted the responsibility of providing schooling for all persons of Native ancestry following Davin's recommendations in 1879. Davin's report focussed on the northwest but excluded Manitoba. Davin urged that both Status Indians and mixed-bloods be educated in order to provide them with the skills needed to assure them a better future. In 1932, L'Association des Métis de l'Alberta (which later became the Métis Association of Alberta), was formed to draw the government's attention to the plight of the Métis of that province (MacEwan, 1981: 141). Also in 1932, Charles Parker, Inspector for the Indian Agencies in the Mackenzie District, urged that government leaders pay heed to the unfortunate living conditions among the "half-breeds of the north." He saw the Métis as poor outcasts, victims of one of the most iniquitous schemes ever fostered and maliciously operated, who should be awarded the full privileges of Status Indians. Ten years later, some Métis in the Mackenzie were added to the respective treaty list on the basis they were economically much worse off than Status Indians. Even then, coupled with other parallel efforts, the future of the Métis depended on the collective will and determination of the people themselves to find solutions and bring about needed change (Fumoleau, 1973: 272).

In evaluating Canadian Indian and Métis education in the last century it is helpful to maintain a national perspective of happenings across the nation. Public education was generally non-existent in the west at the beginning of the twentieth century, although Manitoba passed a *School Attendance Act* in 1916, which made school attendance compulsory for children aged 5 to 14. David J. Goggin, Superintendent of Education for the Territories (which at that time included Alberta and Saskatchewan), engineered the formulation of a public system of education during his years of office from 1883 to 1912. Previous to this time public education in Canada had adopted certain distinguishable marks and wrestled with the issues of organization, philosophy, and financing (Patterson, Chalmers and Friesen, 1974: 98). Most of the advances in education hardly affected the Native population except for those Métis who chose to enter the Canadian mainstream through integration or assimilation.

An evaluation of schooling in Manitoba in 1938 revealed that most schools operating in Native communities were under religious jurisdiction and their teachers had inadequate training. Much of the curriculum emphasis was on religion to the detriment of the academic subjects (Sealey, 1980: 34). A parallel development was the "orphan school" developed by C.K. Rogers, a senior administrator with the Department of Education in Manitoba from 1928 to 1959. Each spring, any surplus money from a supply budget was put into a special fund and used to send teachers to remote areas to teach in the orphan schools. Those participating included unemployed teachers and university students. No school buildings were available to the teachers so a variety of other facilities was used. The curriculum offered minimal instruction in the three "r's," no inspectors visited the schools, and apparently no records were kept. The orphan schools were closed after World War II when the province was able to finance the extension of its public system further north (Sealey, 1980: 45).

The road to universal public education in the northern regions of the prairie provinces was often fraught with complex conditions.

During the 1940s, unless religious denominations provided them, many northern districts did not even have schools. As late as the early 1960s there were still many mission schools operating across the prairie provinces. This situation prevailed partially because of the difficulty in establishing a public system. In Alberta, for example, there were three requirements for the establishment of a school district including: (i) at least eight school-age children had to be resident in the proposed district; (ii) enough assessable, deeded land had to be registered to provide a tax base to raise the necessary revenue; and, (iii) the consent of the majority of taxpayers in said district had to be rendered. The second criterion was the most difficult to meet because much northern occupied land was not owned by individuals and therefore could not be taxed. As a result residents were neither owners nor electors and they could not have established a school district if they had wanted to (Chalmers, 1977).

Towards Formal School Systems

Saskatchewan

After the Second World War many social changes in Canada came about, particularly in regard to education. In 1939, Saskatchewan's N.L. Reid of the province's Department of Education surveyed the educational situation of the province's northern regions but his report was filed and forgotten until after the war. Another study, conducted five years later, suggested the establishment of a special northern school district to meet the needs of northern dwellers, particularly the Métis. The task was ultimately undertaken and although local advisory groups were arranged for, administrative power lay with the Northern Education Committee which was responsible to the Minister of Education.

Very early in the operation of the new school board it was reported that additional school buildings and teacher residences had been built and equipped, and old ones repaired. Better qualified teachers were hired and pupil enrollment more than doubled (Knill and Davies, 1966: 202). Another base for later developments was a proposal in 1959, by Métis leader, Jim Brady, on behalf of the Lac La Ronge School District in which he laid out a series of major proposals for educational development in the north including: (i) equality of education for Native people, even if costs were high; (ii) rigorous enforcement of compulsory education among Native peoples; (iii) educational training for citizenship including instruction in student self-government; (iv) adult education courses for basic literacy; and, (v) the establishment of a special selection apparatus for northern teaching appointments (Dobbin, 1981: 208).

More than a decade passed before Brady's suggestions were examined. Finally, in 1972, the Saskatchewan provincial government created the Department of Northern Saskatchewan with a branch Northern School Board, presently known as Northern Lights School Division #113. Today the responsibility of the division is solely in the area of Native education and in its initial efforts this body has managed to improve transportation facilities and health services and formulate effective conservation policies. When the government initiated this body, it acted on the basis of three previously-approved objectives: (i) to give all northern children the best possible educational opportunities; (ii) to extend the educational program into the community by encouraging local participation and responsibility; and, (iii) to encourage residents of communities to accept increasing responsibility for the operation of their schools (Knill and Davies, 1966: 287-288).

At present the Northern Lights School Division is committed to serving Cree, Dene, Métis, and EuroCanadian cultures and operates 26 schools with student populations ranging from 12 to 500 students per school. Division administrators insist they are progressively piloting programs unique to Canada, by staying on the cutting edge of technology, and integrating the cultural aspects of the varied communities they serve in the classrooms.

Alberta

In the later 1950s, school administrators in Alberta who were responsible for managing federal schools found they had a shortage of space, and simply could not accommodate nonStatus or Métis children in their schools. These children were after all the responsibility of the Provincial Department of Education. Established independent northern school districts were also clamoring for space and denominational schools were struggling with a usual shortage of funds. With federal encouragement, administrators who were aware that they did not legally have to accommo-

date nonStatus students in their schools, approached the province
to assume their legal responsibility. Yielding to legal logic, the
province assigned the responsibility for educating Métis children
to the Provincial Department of Education. The previous practice,
albeit not completely satisfactory, was that the federal government
charged the provincial government a tuition fee for each nonStatus
or Métis student enrolled in their schools.

Soon additional provincial school districts were designed in
northern Alberta, for example, at Grouard, Wabasca, and Trout
Lake, for a total of 20 districts in operation by the fall of 1960
(Chalmers, 1984: 5). By the end of the year, on December 30, 1960,
the province had established the Northland School Division under
the leadership of a three-person board. The new district also took
in Métis colony schools with the exception of Paddle Prairie which
joined the Vermilion School District. The innovative Northland system included a student body of over 2 300 children whose previous
school experiences included mission, Indian, public and Métis
colony schools. According to Chalmers' definition of Métis, almost
half of the student body (1 265 students) were Métis (Ledgerwood,
1972: 16).

The Northland School Division began with a very simple
administrative structure and operated according to a flexible policy. No one was permitted to refer to the previous year's minutes in
resolving problems. Moreover, the government gave administrators a freer hand in finances; funds, once granted to Northland,
could not be recalled nor re-allocated to any other educational
activity. Observers called the Northland Division the "Moose
Division" because it was "big, awkward and went like hell"
(Chalmers, 1977).

In 1961, the federal and provincial governments signed an
agreement to build vocational schools in northern districts on a
shared cost basis. The Northland School Division opened such a
school in Grouard and accepted students who were in grades eight
or nine, but maintained its primary objective of job training. It was
hoped that school graduates would be able to obtain jobs in northern Native settlements so that they would not find it necessary to
relocate to larger, more southerly centres. By 1963, other school districts further south adopted this practice as well and discovered

that the program attracted many non-academic nonNative students as well (Chalmers, 1967: 278-279). This format of education was initiated on the platform of educational integration which was seen as an irreversible and effective process. As discussed earlier, educational integration was simultaneously being promulgated in First Nations' communities.

In 1965, the Province of Alberta passed an act of legislation specifically for the Northland School Division to be managed by a government-appointed board. Initially reports were that the new school division started off on a solid base but within a decade there were rumblings of concern and discontent. Administrators and legislators worked hard to alleviate arising tensions and despite rough times, succeeded in developing a workable northern school division. Today, the Northland School Division is managed by ten staff administrators servicing 23 schools in an area highlighted by five major water systems, covering a 250 000 square metre area.

Manitoba

Following the example of the two more westerly provinces, Manitoba eventually addressed the subject of Métis education as well. Earlier, in 1947, a special committee had been appointed by the Manitoba government to enquire into Hutterite education. The supervisor of the project energetically travelled the northern regions of the province, through remote communities, evaluating educational conditions. After completing their evaluation the committee identified very poor educational conditions and urged rapid action in their report. To their credit, the government responded quickly.

In 1957 the Supervisor of Special Schools was assigned to administrate 35 schools comprising a total of 100 classrooms of students (Sealey, 1980: 47). Two years later a report was issued by the provincial Social and Economic Research Office on behalf of the Department of Agriculture and Immigration regarding the living conditions of the Manitoba population of Indian ancestry. In examining the special school situation the framers of the report indicated that the supervisor had too heavy a workload which should be adjusted and more supervisory staff should be hired. It was also reported that the most significant achievement in terms of Métis education was the fact that children were attending school in larger numbers than in previous years. However, the dropout rate was still very high and the average leaving grade was 5.84 (Lagasse, 1959, Vol. 1: 128).

The report completed by the Department of Agriculture and Immigration encompassed three volumes and surveyed Métis people from a variety of life situations. Surveyors examined the living conditions of Métis communities situated on the fringe of Indian reserves, those living on the edges of nonNative settlements, and those living in predominantly Métis communities. They also spent time in Métis settlements near predominantly EuroCanadian communities and those which were not accessible by roads along the northern railway lines. Researchers estimated that 80 percent of Manitoba's Métis were not included in the study because they would already have integrated into dominant society to the point of not being recognized as having Native heritage (Lagasse, 1959, Vol. 1: 77).

A number of concerns emanated from the Manitoba report, particularly the high dropout rate of Métis students. Reasons for leaving school were not surprising, and students who were surveyed included these reasons: had to go to work, had to stay home and help, got tired of school, or did not like school, further schooling not available, could not afford to go, had an illness (Lagasse, 1959, Vol. II: 53-56). Five factors were identified that hindered Métis education and the Department of Education was urged to rectify them. Factors included: (i) education could not be delivered to isolated communities situated too far away from accessible roadways; (ii) age-grade retardation; (iii) lack of attendance related to age-grade retardation; (iv) administration and supervision problems; and, (v) the need for remedial services (Lagasse, 1959, Vol. III: 121).

The Manitoba report concluded with a number of significant recommendations urging improved school facilities, better qualified teachers, enhanced financing, stronger measures of enforcement for school attendance, and the provision of remedial services. The report recommended that more permanent kinds of job opportunities for Métis breadwinners would discourage the nomadic way of life and encourage improved school attendance on the part of the children. Finally, the report encouraged an integrated form of education, mixing Métis with nonNative children in provincial schools so that the attitudes and morals of the EuroCanadian society would be more readily inculcated by Métis children (Lagasse, 1959, Vol. III: 132-133).

The committee report reflected the general trend in Native education policy fostered by the federal Department of Indian Affairs Branch which, since 1949, had fostered an integrated form of education. The concept was that with this format, Native children would better be prepared to take their places as full-fledged Canadian citizens. (Brookes, 1991: 49-51). The federal government was adamant that "integration should not be confused, either in the minds of the Indian people, or the public at large, with assimilation" (Daniels, 1967: 28).

In 1963, a number of Manitoba's senior governmental officers and advisors travelled to northern Alberta to meet with the administrators of the Northland School Division and visit some of the division's schools. They also studied the Saskatchewan arrangement and, in 1965, under Bill No. 47, created the Frontier School Division to operate under a single administrator. The initial aims of the new school division included: (i) the upgrading of school facilities and teacher accommodations; (ii) establishment of a high school to serve the needs of the constituency; and, (iii) improvement of instruction (Sealey and Kirkness, 1973: 143).

Within five years the new Manitoba Division had hired 250 teachers to educate 5 000 nonNative students. The Division administration then purchased a former airforce base at Cranberry Portage, renovated it, and developed a residential high school. Thus, for the first time, Métis students in the northern and isolated regions of the province had available to them a secondary school with numerous options. In its first year (1965) the school attracted 189 students and by 1972 the enrollment was 701. Most of the students occupied dormitories at the Cranberry School, while others were billeted in private homes (Sealey, 1980: 49). This option again reflected the general Indian education policy adopted by the federal government through the Education Division of the Department of Indian Affairs, which tended to filter down in slightly modified form to provincial systems.

Complications

The establishment of northern school systems in the Prairie Provinces did not immediately resolve all educational problems nor provide completely effective schooling to all areas. In many settlements the challenge of adequate education was primarily economic, not pedagogical. Many residents in the northern areas earned only meagre wages and often had to leave home for seasonal employment elsewhere. This necessity adversely affected family life. Researchers found that as self-sufficiency disappeared, so did the feeling of self-respect (Sealey and Lussier, 1975: 185). Education, if it was to be effective in this context, would have to incorporate the development of student self-esteem and social wellbeing. Many more ambitious individuals left their northern communities and migrated to more active northern centres or to larger towns and cities further south. However, unless those persons had the wherewithal to cope in urban settings, socially as well as in terms of the job market, they often found themselves lonely enough to want to return home accompanied by feelings of failure and without any prospects of employment on arrival home.

In 1972, the Manitoba Métis Federation prepared a document entitled, In Search of a Future, focussing attention on the challenges faced by Métis migrants in urban centres (Fulham, 1972). The report urged a government study to assess the economic viability of northern communities from where the migrants originated. The attainment of better education in isolated communities also implied the need for job placement after graduation. Another concern identified by the report was the adjustment process undergone by urban-migrating Métis, many of whom faced a complexity of personal problems after their relocation. The report also recommended the establishment of a series of migration centres to assist Métis in dealing with the challenges of relocation and job preparation (Sealey and Lussier, 1975: 187).

First Case Study: Fort Chipewyan, Alberta

As though economic complications were not enough, the newly-developed northern prairie school systems soon encountered unforseen challenges which dampened the original enthusiasm of their promoters. This was amply demonstrated by development in the Northland School Division in Alberta. An evaluation of the Division a decade after its formulation revealed that while school enrollments had originally burgeoned, by the early 1970s the student population remained at a steady level. When the standards of achievement were compared with provincial schools, there was severe age-grade differences, particularly at the primary levels. Although this unfortunate situation decreased dramatically in the initial decade, the dropout rate was still a cause for alarm. High school enrollment figures were low, and though even more students were enrolled in the upper grades, educators became concerned about the potentially dismal prospects faced by school graduates. Coupled with the fact of low employment opportunities in northern communities there was evidence that the school system was not adequately preparing students to face the limitations of the local job market or what to expect if they found it necessary to take up residence elsewhere.

In addition to pedagogical challenges, the Northland School Division also had problems of an administrative nature. After a decade of "free spirit" operation, bureaucracy set in, and the flush of enthusiasm posited by the first administrators was replaced by management-oriented government bureaucrats who were more interested in setting budgets and cost-efficiency measures than pedagogy. These officials were anxious to hold the line on costs when they realized the enormity of expense connected to operating northern schools (Chalmers, 1972, 1977). It was also difficult to build up a stable teaching staff in Northland because of the remoteness of many of the schools and the undesirability of locating to these communities without relevant prior teaching experience. Teachers who did sign contracts with Northland encountered a variety of unexpected complications such as teaching a curriculum that was somewhat irrelevant, since it was geared to life in EuroCanadian urban communities, coping with teaching English as a second language, and learning how to survive in often isolated communities amidst extremely cold temperatures.

MacNeil Commission

In 1981, an Alberta provincial study undertaken by the MacNeil Commission identified a series of important problems for northern teachers. A primary concern was teacher turn-over, which sometimes reached 50 percent annually. The reasons teachers gave for disillusionment with northern teaching included a lack of preparation time, multi-grade classrooms, low levels of pupil achievement, and a number of factors connected with living in relatively isolated areas. A second concern identified by the Commission related to the perceptions which Northland teachers had of the operations of the Northland School Division. Teachers felt that the board was not interested in developing good school-community relations and the board explicitly discouraged teachers from becoming too friendly with local residents. Generally, the Commission found that teacher morale was low and teachers felt that community perceptions of their profession were not very gratifying. They believed that their ideas were not really welcomed by the board and they feared punitive actions if they criticized the board or expressed dissatisfaction with working conditions (MacNeil, 1981: 31-32).

Local Survey

In 1981 a survey of local community residents in Fort Chipewyan, Alberta, one of the communities hosting a Northland Division School, revealed a number of problems connected to the local education milieu. The research work was carried out by a group of local citizens who were enrolled in extension courses offered by the University of Calgary's Native Outreach Program. The study made note of several positive characteristics of the local schooling format, notably the fact that a local newspaper had been initiated by the school, traditional Native skills and crafts were being taught in the off-hours of school operation, and substitute teachers were being hired from among local citizens who had knowledge of local workings even if their educational qualifications were not up to provincial standards. This was especially appreciated by the teaching administration who had experienced difficulty in obtaining the assistance of substitute teachers in the past. Community residents were enthused about enhanced student achievement over the years that the Northland School had operated and expressed appreciation about the efforts of school staff who encouraged parent-community involvement (Friesen and Boberg, 1990: 151).

According to study results, Fort Chipewyan schools came under fire in terms of failing to maintain academic standards, neglecting to include relevant subject matter about Native history and culture in the curriculum, and "turning out an inferior product in so far as the job market was concerned." Students wishing to complete high school had to relocate to other northern centres such as Fort Smith or Fort McMurray where all twelve grades of schooling were offered. Many who did so soon returned home because they found living away from home too intimidating. Also, since local jobs were scarce, critics felt that schooling did little to prepare students for the reality of the situation. Thus the only realistic expectation of the school was basic literacy, and even then it offered only a substandard form of delivery and limited socialization (Friesen and Boberg, 1990: 151).

A resolution of Fort Chipewyan's schooling dilemma landed in the laps of three parties – government, local educational personnel, and the community. The fact was, however, that the provincial Department of Education was responsible for providing adequate education for all of the province's children. Realistically, this could mean that the same form of education would be provided in every community with some adaptation to local needs.

During the discussion of study results it was pointed out that in northern regions there are many economic implications concerning schooling. For example, people who complete their schooling must also find work, preferably in their home communities. The educational challenge in settlements like Fort Chipewyan therefore concern policy, curriculum, and teaching staff. The stability of the teaching staff has finally been attained, partially aided by an unrelated and somewhat dubious factor, namely the past shortage of jobs for teachers. The move towards local control on the part of Native peoples has also provided a measure of stability and encouraged concern about the relevancy of school curricula in Native communities. School policy, however, must still be modified to reflect local needs.

Local School Boards

Things came to a head in Northland after the MacNeil Commission reported and within a few years significant changes were incepted. Among its recommendations the Commission opted for elected school board members rather than their being appointed by the Minister of Education as was the tradition. A Northland School Division Investigative Committee was set up to send surveyors to every Northland school community to determine what citizens wanted in terms of schooling in their communities. The committee was to determine what the community's conceptualizations of and preferences for schooling might be. After the investigation was completed an entirely new form of educational administration was initiated. A new *Northland School Division Act* passed on June 6, 1983 (Bill No. 58), gave all eligible residents of each community with an operating school board provision to elect a three to seven person local school board committee. Each of these school boards were then to elect a chairperson who became a member of the Board of Trustees of the Northland School Division and representative of the local area. This board now has the same powers and responsibilities of every other school board in Alberta. At the time of inception the Northland School Division operated 26 schools, hired 193 teachers, and enrolled some 2 500 students.

Second Case Study: Camperville, Manitoba

The establishment of workable schools in northern areas has occasionally encountered another obstacle in the form of prejudice, discrimination, and unfair treatment, particularly in integrated situations. A 1973 case study of Camperville, Manitoba drove this point home (Sealey, 1977). At that time the children of Camperville, a Métis community of 700 residents located 300 kilometres north of Winnipeg and 50 kilometres north of Winnipegosis, were bussed to Winnipegosis to complete their high school. There they were faced with what community residents knew to be a long-standing campaign of racism and inequity. A local elementary school in Camperville also failed to meet the needs of the Métis population since it was typical of urban nonNative schools elsewhere in the province, both in terms of curriculum content and school objectives. Native subject matter was noticeably absent in school curriculum, and the purpose of schooling was specifically oriented towards nonNative values.

A protest was launched on March 15, 1973, and parents of the Métis children conducted a sit-in at the local school. They presented a list of 22 grievances to the school principal and demanded their resolution. The major concerns were alleged prejudice on the part of nonNative teachers towards Métis students, cultural discrimination in regard to forms of dress, racial taunts and insults from Winnipegosis nonNative students and a lack of relevance in the school curriculum which completely omitted any reference to Métis history and culture (Sealey, 1977: 152).

After fruitless local exchange regarding the format for negotiations, the Manitoba Minister of Education was contacted, resulting in his sending two officials to investigate the incident. Student grievances were then referred to the Provincial Human Rights Commission whose targeted investigation focussed on nine alleged infractions of Métis rights. The first infraction pertained to bussing problems to the collegiate, because Métis students were transported home immediately at the end of the school day and thus, unlike resident Winnipegosis students, could not make use of school facilities after school hours.

The Human Rights Commission also found incidents of racism on the part of nonNative students, teachers, and townspeople, particularly towards young Métis girls who were often the object of racist taunts and obscenities by some men in the community. The melting-pot orientation of both schools was targeted, and it was noted that while these institutions were oriented to a nonNative middle-class lifestyle, the curriculum made absolutely no mention of Métis history and culture. As a result of these and other conditions in all the years that Camperville children had attended high school in Winnipegosis only six students had completed Grade 12 and even then some of them did not pass all Grade 12 departmental exams.

The Human Rights Commission investigated the alleged improprieties and after appropriate investigation issued a report. It was acknowledged that Métis students were not being served by the educational program in place at that time. Indeed the dropout rate for Métis high school students was 96%, most of them occurring in Grade nine. This was happening during a time when most nonNative Winnipegosis students were graduating from high school. In addition, Métis students entering the local collegiate were one full grade behind their nonNative counterparts on the Canadian Test of Basic Skills.

The Commission found definite evidence of prejudice and discrimination toward the Métis. It also noted that the nonNative middle-class orientation of both schools, elementary and collegiate, ignored Native history. This was the case despite the fact that the elementary school student population in Camperville was 95% Métis and the Winnipegosis collegiate had a 28% Métis population. No effort was made on the part of school staff to recognize the socio-cultural needs of the Métis students, for example, the fact that in the average Camperville home there was no adequate place for students to study because of the very cramped quarters. In general, the atmosphere of the collegiate was to "look down upon Métis students" and the school did not clearly reflect a policy of social integration. Part of the solution posed by the Human Rights Commission was to seek the cooperation of the Camperville and other nearby Métis communities in building a local high school in Camperville. Another concern was to help the local school district in developing a cross-cultural component in the school curriculum that would take cognizance of Native history and culture (Sealey, 1977: 156-157).

The end results of the Camperville investigation were disappointing to say the least. Some changes were effected in the areas specified and a principal who had some knowledge of Aboriginal ways was hired to administrate the Camperville Elementary School. In addition, some cross-cultural training for local teaching staff was made available. A special counsellor at the collegiate was instructed to spend additional time with Métis students and a more positive attitude towards Métis students in the school environment gradually became apparent. The local high school in Camperville never did materialize and Métis students continued to attend high school in Winnipegosis. A decade later, with little or no change in conditions, on April 16, 1984, 350 Métis in Camperville declared themselves an independent nation. They designed and flew a flag declaring absolute jurisdiction over their landspace covering some 500 square kilometres. A primary reason for this move was to attract attention to the Métis desire for self-government. The provincial government ignored the event and within a few days so did the media (Purich, 1988: 158). The situation represents only one of many futile attempts by Native people to try to draw national attention to very unfortunate circumstances.

Analysis

Those students of Métis educational history who look for solutions may be challenged by a Saskatchewan study conducted by the late Howard Adams which concluded that, all other things being equal, Métis students benefit less from public education than their nonNative counterparts because of: (i) low aspirations; (ii) an inadequate concept of education; and, (iii) social discrimination (Adams, 1972: 30-31). Bruce Sealey of the Manitoba Métis Federation discovered two additional factors: (iv) an inadequate self-concept; and, (v) a lack of academic tradition in the family (Sealey, 1977: 162). Add to this a lavish dose of parental apathy brought about by unemployment and disillusionment with their own poor academic records; then combine this with poor student work habits, and educational failure is almost guaranteed (Lussier and Sealey, 1978, Vol. II: 151-152).

Métis educators, Lussier and Sealey, have analyzed the attitudes of teachers working in Native communities with the conclusion that many educators often function according to a series of faulty assumptions. First, educators often assume that their students will be unable to function in dominant society without attaining the educational skills which the regular system offers. This is true only if such students involve themselves in life situations where the skills that are taught in provincial schools are required. Students returning to their home communities will not likely find that their educational accomplishments will be of much relevance or applicability.

Second, teachers sometimes employ the term "outside world" when they speak of educational philosophy, as though such a concept is nonexistent in a Native setting. For these educators education in a large urban arena to which it is usually geared, falls into a neat perspective and ties in with the economic base of urban centres. As a result these teachers are unable to think, react, or effectively function within parameters which differ in what they perceive as basic fundamentals (Lussier and Sealey, 1978, Vol. II: 144-245). The result is often frustration, professional dissatisfaction or relocation.

The concept of preparing Native teachers for Native classrooms has been given lip service in western Canadian universities for at least two decades (Friesen, 1985: 42). Following the example of other pioneer institutions, like the University of Saskatchewan and Brandon University, the University of Calgary initiated its Native Outreach Program in 1972. The concept was to provide the first two or three years of teacher education on site in Native communities, and have student complete their degree programs on campus. Early experiments revealed severe difficulties for program participants, particularly with regard to the final year(s) when students were required to relocate to the urban university campus. Often unequipped for big city life with all of its vicissitudes, and often lonely, some returned home instead of finishing their programs of study (Friesen, 1991b: 230).

For some years the University of Regina and the University of Saskatchewan in conjunction with the Gabriel Dumont Institute of Native Studies and Applied Research have sponsored the Saskatchewan Urban Native Teacher Education Program and discovered that urban adjustment on the part of incoming rural-based Indian and Métis students was often a tough challenge. As a result educators devised a support group concept which incorporated a variety of campus structures and events to help such students keep in touch with one another and so bolster their motivation for remaining in the program. This process began with first enrollment and continued after graduation while working in the field. Graduates were also invited back to help with the orientation of first-year students where they stressed the importance of Indian/Métis identity and the importance of the "group" to personal success (Lang and Scarfe, 1985).

As the movement toward local control of education flourishes in First Nations and Métis communities we will undoubtedly witness significant parallel changes in schooling. Such a move would be indicative of the general Métis "return to roots" movement that has either been underground for too long it is only now becoming visible to the nonNative world (Dorion and Préfontaine, 2001: 14). In the meanwhile, the Manitoba Métis Federation has staked a land claim to the Red River forks in Winnipeg as well as to the downtown core of the city which they believe they were cheated out of 120 years ago. They also insist that Louis Riel be honored as a Father of Confederation. If this is a visible sign of the rising crescendo of Métis identity, the provision of fair and effective schooling can only fuel the fires of Métis nationalism. Indeed the reality is coming to be, as stated prophetically by Augustine Abraham, a descendant of Louis Riel, "... [today] it is fashionable to be Métis" (Robertson, 1992: 102).

7

Intensification

It is all too easy, should disturbances erupt, to crush them in the name of law and order. We must never forget that, in the long run, a democracy is judged by the way the majority treats the minority. Louis Riel's battle is not yet won. – Pierre Elliott Trudeau, Prime Minister of Canada, in an address at the unveiling of the Louis Riel Monument in Regina, Saskatchewan, October 2, 1969, italics ours (Colombo, 1987: 327).

The culturally based Medicine Wheel Nursery School [in Calgary] opened in March [2003] and combines Alberta Learning curriculum with education in traditional Métis values and culture....if we can give them [Métis children] a sense of belonging, they'll be better prepared to be out in the world and be proud of who they are. (*Calgary Herald*, Saturday, May 3, 2003: B1)

As the Métis continue to devote their energies towards defining their role in Canada's future, there are a number of very complex confronting situations with which they will have to deal. On the positive side, the Supreme Court of Canada has chosen to validate their claims; the Métis are now legally recognized as Aboriginal people in Canada. In order to ensure equal representation, there is some indication that attention will have to be given to the matter of guaranteeing Aboriginal representation in a newly-conceived senate, perhaps by an individual from within the Native community. In addition, deals like the 1990 arrangement with the Province of Alberta to transfer 500 000 hectares of land, plus 310 million dollars in cash to residents of eight pre-existing rural Métis settlements will allow the Métis freedom to carry on their traditional lifestyle. Unlike federal reserve arrangements, the Métis set-up allows for change and anticipates eventual self-sufficiency on the part of the Métis communities. For example, an individual Métis with land title must improve it within five years or lose title. In addition, title holders must pay an annual levy to support Métis governments.

The supreme court decision affecting land claims could change all that.

The federal government is currently working on a three-way deal called the Tripartite Cooperative Agreement which will assure self-government for the Alberta Métis. The government has already funnelled $600 000 into the initiative to launch consultative meetings to encourage local participation (*The Native Network News,* August, 1992). Finally, there is hope in the field of education as the various provincial departments of education have recognized the distinctiveness of Métis children's needs and tried to adjust curriculum concerns accordingly.

The Tripartite Agreement is viewed by Métis leaders as a way to encourage Métis pride and self-reliance. The agreement guarantees a degree of certainty in proposed constitutional changes and will, hopefully, be augmented by later actions in that regard. Supplementing this, is the country's commitment to a policy on multiculturalism which states that the federal government will promote policies that guarantee equality of opportunity for all citizens. The government is committed to originating and revising policies that will operationalize access to government services for all citizens and encourage the preservation of the linguistic, cultural and religious heritages of all Canadians. The government will encourage policies that facilitate the preservation of heritages of all citizens and recognize the contribution of all members of society even to the point of providing assistance in clarifying for the public, government policies relating to multiculturalism (Friesen, 1991c: 243-244). If the Métis people choose a form of multiculturalism, over the path of assimilation, they have the right to expect governmental support to pursue this approach (Roberts, von Below, and Bos, 2001: 197). Against this background it would appear that the preservation of Métis culture and identity will have ample formal support. Two bigger challenges will be to unite the Métis into one nationhood, and also gain public awareness of and approval for the fact that Métis legal status has changed.

A brief review of the evolutionary history of the Métis people predates the legitimacy of their legal claims. Over the last four decades the Métis have worked hard to develop a national consciousness and acquire a strong degree of cohesiveness as a people.

They have a good historical foundation for these claims. As far back as 1816, under the leadership of Cuthbert Grant, they rose in armed protest against economic sanctions placed by the Hudson's Bay Company on the sale of pemmican. Many Métis annually celebrate the Métis victory at "La Grenouillere" with the singing of a "national hymn." Commonly referred to as the Battle of Seven Oaks in the Canadian historical record, it was also the event at which the Métis designed and flew their first flag. The trial of Guillaume Sayer in 1849 provided another opportunity for the Métis to lay a claim to fame when they successfully challenged the authority of the principal fur trading company. The monopoly was finally broken by this action, and the company's local political authority, the Assiniboia Council, never regained its governing stronghold (Payment, 1990: 21).

The accumulated historical pluses garnered by the Métis over the last century has given them ample cause to see themselves as a "new nation" with a separate and valid identity in the Northwest. This was Riel's dream. The Métis cultural perspective can proceed even though it fosters some degree of heterogeneity (Foster, 2001). The "Métis Indians," who descended from English-speaking peoples, tend to follow Native ways. The French Métis, on the other hand, share a common language and faith, and a stable kinship network tied to two or three generations of residence in the Northwest. Though their numbers reflect several socioeconomic classes, derived from their occupations, their common bonds of cultural heritage and religion assure a degree of solidarity (Payment, 1990). Against this background it must be recognized that the charisma of Louis has continued to fuel Métis nationalism to the point that its century-long echo can now become reality.

The Multicultural Challenge

The move to include Métis culture in the Canadian mosaic via the fundamentals of multiculturalism is underway. However, the principles of multiculturalism are just that; they are principles, not policy, not programs, and not practice. Generalizing the objectives of multiculturalism on a national scale in a country as diverse as Canada is a complex matter, even when the universally-accepted values of freedom of speech, justice, and the guarantee of equality of opportunity are legally assured. Thus it is no mean task to be able to fully access the privileges of a legal cultural mosaic, and Métis leaders have certainly become aware of this. This challenge has also proven to be a difficult arena for Status Indians as well even though they can point to extraordinary legislation passed on their behalf. They can legally claim the right of first occupancy and point to the geographic specialty of always having consistently occupied this continent – unlike the more recently arrived Europeans. Moreover, First Nations cultures are significantly different from that of dominant society in that they regard nature as primary and see technological advances in a corollary context (Friesen, 1995). Even legally, the First Nations have been targeted for special attention in ample legislation that sets them apart from the rest of society (Berry, 1991). However, even in light of these strong considerations, it can still be argued that Native cultures in Canada have not received much by way of cultural appreciation on the part of their fellow Canadians.

If the Status Indians of Canada have difficulty in gaining recognition as a distinct culture by their Canadian peers, their Métis counterparts face an even tougher challenge. Canadian multiculturalism, which is intended to recognize, respect, and even encourage diversity is a recent phenomenon. Like the Aboriginal peoples, every immigrant ethnocultural community, from the date of their arrival, has been the target of assimilation to the Anglomono culture using schooling as the main instrument. A slight deviation was observable in the 1870s when Canada competed with the United States for immigrants. At that time, large blocks of land were set aside for incoming groups who were told that they could build their "ethnocultural ghettos" on them – just like back home (House, 1992). Before long, however, in 1892, in fact, the North West Territories passed an ordinance giving the government complete control of education. The ordinance did away with the denominational board of education, which had operated since 1884, and introduced a political Council of Public Instruction. The Premier, F. W. Haultain, then invited David J. Goggin to become the new schools system's first superintendent. Goggin was hired to bring uniformity and harmony to the system, and he followed the lead of the premier who wanted to abolish the "Protestant and Catholic antagonism in politics, education and social life, and endeavor to unite the people in one bond of national ideas" (McDonald, 1974: 173).

David Goggin was a nationalist imperialist who identified strongly with the Anglo-Saxon WASP community of nineteenth century Canada. His dream was to gather the children of the many creeds, races, and customs into a common school and "Canadianize" them. He believed that Canadian children should grow up and "adopt our viewpoint and speak our speech." The perspective which he advanced was unequivocally and emphatically British. In Regina, at the occasion of Queen Victoria's Diamond Jubilee in 1887, at which he was a speaker, Goggin enjoined his listeners to "halt and thank God for an Empire, the most splendid possession ever entrusted to any people" (McDonald, 1974: 177). He did not agree with assigning special status to any group, particularly the French, not because they were Roman Catholic (which he was not), but because they were French. Along with the French, whom he designated as "non-English," Goggin included Swedes, Finns, Bohemians, Hungarians, Jews, Austrians, Germans, Russians, Icelanders, Mennonites, Galacians, Doukhobors, and all other ethnic groups. If Aboriginal communities like the Métis had any hopes of gaining a hearing for special needs in education, their claims were certain to fall on deaf ears.

Canada does not have an admirable record with regard to the treatment of the nation's ethnic minorities, including Aboriginal peoples. The underlying reality is that no minority can access any rights, even legislated rights, without majority approval. In the legislative context it is at the same time recognized that the presence of a very strong opposition guarantees and safeguards minority rights, and serves as a watchdog to ensure that the democratic majority does not misuse its power. One might even go so far as to say that when decisions are made by the majority, the minority may have to go along with them, but they do not have to like them (Friesen, 1977: 27). Moreover, they have the privilege and legal right to work against such decisions with the eventual hope that they may be overturned. This assumes that the process of democratic representation is available to the minority in question, but this is not necessarily a reality when certain ethnic groups have little representation in the legislature (Friesen, 1985: 34).

Legislation notwithstanding, there are other fronts on which Canada's Métis people will continue to struggle well into the twenty-first century. A primary concern will be to achieve a measure of internal unity in order to present a solidarity front to their Canadian neighbors.

Internal Struggles

Adams (1999: 131) charges that one of the greatest threats to Native political success in Canada is neocolonialism, a process by which a corrupt class of Aboriginals profits at the expense of the majority. His argument is that as federal and provincial governments have provided large funds for the operation of national Aboriginal agencies and organizations, their leaders have taken advantage of the situation and spent money on themselves, ignoring the needs of their people. Apparently, even universities contribute to the problem. Universities which house Native studies departments too often foster neocolonialism by educating the Native elite to fill the role abandoned by government bureaucrats (Adams, 1999: 54).

There are many subcategories within the Aboriginal community which sometimes cause social or political divisions among them. The Métis community contained two significant subsections from its beginning, namely those who had French ancestors, who were best known as Métis, and those with English bloodlines (half-breeds), who were later called nonStatus First Nations. The passing of the first Indian Act in 1876 provided legal recognition for Indian people who later became known as Registered or Status Indians. Many were left out or ignored due to poor administrative operations. The signing of the numbered treaties in the 1870s created further distinctions, since many Aboriginals in British Columbia and northern Quebec were not party to treaty-signing. Since then the terms, "Registered-Treaty" and "Registered-nonTreaty" have developed special meanings.

There are also differences in the way the various treaty groups have dealt with government. Until very recently, Native people in Alberta worked together within the parameters of the Indian Association of Alberta which incorporated both Indian and Métis concerns. When that organization wound up its office in October,

1992, its concerns were assigned to three treaty groups, numbers six, seven, and eight. Here too, there are differences in representation; for example, treaty seven tribes are all resident in southern Alberta while Treaty Eight tribes live in three different provinces – British Columbia, Alberta, and Saskatchewan.

In recent decades as Native people have migrated to the cities, the designations, "on-reserve and off-reserve" First Nations have also gained significance (Frideres and Gadacz, 2001: 24f). In fact, the number of Aboriginals who have moved to urban centres has reached such proportions that many of them have banded together and sought government attention because of their special needs as urban Indians. According to the 1996 census, 79 percent of Canada's 1 101 955 Aboriginal peoples (including Status, nonStatus, Inuit and Métis), lived off-reserve, and this trend is increasing. Some Aboriginal groups who have relocated to urban centres have purchased land for the purpose of corporately pursuing economic opportunities and functioning as an Indian reserve (Friesen and Friesen, 2002: 140).

In every cultural community, there are other unique subcategories which often serve to confound solidarity, that is, bloodlines, family connections, clan linkages, and political affiliations. As the legal process of reinstating previously disenfranchised individuals continues, because of the stipulations of Bill C-31, there are also instances where individuals who regain a legally-recognized Indian identity experience difficulties in being accepted by the Status community. In the meantime, since a high degree of prejudice against Native people still exists in Canada, there are individuals who simply refuse to identify themselves as Métis in the Canadian census to avoid discrimination. Naturally, this confuses the actual count of Métis in Canada (Peterson and Brown, 1985).

Future Outlook

Unlike other Aboriginal groups in Canada, the Métis share a mutual respect for their departed hero, Louis Riel. Until September 19, 2003, the nation's eyes were on Ottawa while the supreme court sat in session. That matter seems to have been resolved, but there are also continued pleas for Riel's posthumous pardon. The campaign is a common cause for the Métis and serves to bind them together with the same intensity that charismatic leaders command among their followers. The biblical phrase, "I am he that liveth, and was dead" (Revelation 1:18a King James Version)," certainly applies to Louis Riel.

There are basically two kinds of pardons in Canada: (i) free pardon, which is granted on the grounds of innocence established and admitted by the Crown; and, (ii) pardon which is granted on special consideration. Both pardons proceed from the same source as an act of grace, but the first is an act of grace to which the recipient is morally entitled, while the second is an act of pure grace. The Métis of Canada are breaking ground in requesting a posthumous pardon for Louis Riel, but they believe that the British Crown has the mechanism to grant it. Although representative of the Métis community generally, the Association of Métis and non-Status Indians of Saskatchewan have formulated a list of ten reasons why they believe Louis Riel should be pardoned. Among the points made by the association are arguments that Riel did not seek personal gain with his actions, he committed no illegal act, and he never advocated war. When arrested, he did not receive a just trial and the government ignored the jury's plea for mercy. The government now has an opportunity to heed that plea in pardoning Riel (Association of Métis and non-Status Indians of Saskatchewan, 1979: 85-86).

An affirmation of government commitment to enshrining the memory of Louis Riel through a posthumous pardon could go a long way toward raising the spirits of the Métis towards a renewed vision. Perhaps it would also relegate other concerns such as land claims and legislative recognition to a secondary status. While Métis leaders would appreciate the energizing force of an emotional uplift, which Riel's pardon would provide, they are also prepared to act on their demands. To that end the Manitoba Métis Federation has staked out a land claim at the historic river forks in Winnipeg, including the core of downtown Winnipeg. They also insist that Riel be recognized as a father of Confederation (Robertson, 1992). Like some other minority peoples, they are not content to be just another entity in Canada's multicultural mosaic. As pioneers of multiculturalism, by their very origins, they believe that Métis nationalism is Canadian nationalism. They insist that the place of the Métis in Canada must be articulated on the basis of their being the only charter group in Canada with a history of national political independence before joining Confederation. Other ethnic groups can co-exist with mutual respect within the mainstream of society, but they must also recognize that the Métis are a national and indigenous people, not an ethnic group, largely outside of the mainstream of society (Daniels, 1979: 51).

While the demands of the Métis may appear excessive, they are certainly understandable. It is also worth considering that the Métis position is only a beginning stance in the bargaining process. Even as a starting point, however, their claims have ample historic backing. A multicultural society which espouses and in its very essence fosters extraordinary circumstances, the Métis like other minorities, have a right to expect "extraordinary treatment." A culturally pluralist society implies a form of "inequity" be operant in the quest to provide for the needs of the various subcultures. To be meaningful, the practice of multiculturalism must focus on the special needs of specific minorities, as opposed to overall cultural programming which often only reproduces the cultural hierarchy (Moodley, 1992: 90). The provision for minority needs must, by definition, function according to the principles of sensitivity and flexibility, and even anticipate a form of "inequity" in practice. As thus reality begins to open up for the Métis people, Canadians may finally be able to witness the beginning of rectification in the form of a long overdue justice for the Métis.

References

Adams, Howard. (1972). *The Outsiders.* Saskatoon, SK: Métis Society of Saskatchewan.

Adams, Howard. (1975). *Prison of Grass: Canada From the Native Point of View.* Toronto, ON: New Press.

Adams. Howard. (1999). *Tortured People: The Politics of Colonization.* Revised edition. Penticton, BC: Theytus Books.

Alberta Federation of Métis Settlement Associations and Daniel R. Anderson and Alda M. Anderson. (1978). *The Métis People of Canada: A History.* Edmonton, AB: Syncrude Educational Services.

Anderson, B. (1983). *Imagined Communities: Reflections on the Origin and Spread of Nationalism.* London, UK: Verso.

Anderson, Frank W. (1955).*"1885," The Riel Rebellion.* Calgary, AB: Frontiers Unlimited.

Anderson, Frank W. (1974). *Riel's Manitoba Uprising.* Aldergrove, BC: Frontier Publishing.

Anonymous. (1885). *The Story of Louis Riel: The Rebel Chief.* Toronto, ON: Rose Publishing Company.

Appelbaum, Richard P., and William J. Chambliss. (1995). *Sociology.* New York: Harper Collins College Publishers.

Asch, Michael. (1984). *Home and Native Land: Aboriginal Rights and the Canadian Constitution.* Toronto, ON: Methuen.

Association of Métis and non-Status Indians of Saskatchewan. (1979). *Louis Riel: Justice Must be Done.* Winnipeg. MB: Manitoba Métis Federation Press.

Bakker, Peter. (2001). The Michif Language of the Métis. *Métis Legacy: A Métis Historiography and Annotated Bibliography.* Lawrence J. Barkwell, Leah Dorion, and Darren Préfontaine, eds. Winnipeg, MB: Pemmican Publications, 177-180.

Barkwell, Lawrence, and Ed Swain. (2001). Contributions by Métis People. *Métis Legacy: A Métis Historiography and Annotated Bibliography.* Lawrence J. Barkwell, Leah Dorion, and Darren Préfontaine, eds. Winnipeg, MB: Pemmican Publications, 1-9.

Barkwell, Lawrence J., Leah Dorion, and Darren Préfontaine, eds. (2001). *Métis Legacy: A Métis Historiography and Annotated Bibliography.* Winnipeg, MB: Pemmican Publications.

Barnouw, Victor. (1979). *Anthropology: A General Introduction.* Homewood, IL: The Dorsey Press.

Barron, F. Lauric. (1990). The CCF and the Development of Métis Colonies in Southern Saskatchewan During the Premiership of T. C. Douglas, 1944-1961, *Canadian Journal of Native Studies,* X:2, 243-270.

Benedict, Ruth. (1934). *Patterns of Culture.* New York: Mentor Books.

Berger, Thomas R. (1982). *Fragile Freedoms: Human Rights and Dissent in Canada.* Toronto, ON: Irwin.

Berry, John W. (1991). *Native People and the Larger Society, A Canadian Social Psychology of Ethnic Relations.* Robert C. Gardner and Rudolf Kalin, eds. Toronto, ON: Methuen, 214-230.

Bourgeault, Ron. (1983) Métis History. *One Sky Information Kit: Native People.* Saskatoon, SK: One Sky, 77-85.

Bowsfield, Hartwell. (1971). *Louis Riel: The Rebel and the Hero.* Toronto, ON: Oxford University Press.

Braidwood, Robert J. (1955). *Prehistoric Man, Readings in Anthropology.* E. Adamson Hoebel, Jesse D. Jennings and Elmer R. Smith, eds. New York: McGraw-Hill, 27-35.

Braz, Albert. (2003). *The False Traitor: Louis Riel in Canadian Culture.* Toronto, ON: University of Toronto Press.

Brookes, Sonia. (1991). The Persistence of Native Educational Policy in Canada. *The Cultural Maze: Complex Questions on Native Destiny in Western Canada.* John W. Friesen, ed. Calgary, AB: Detselig Enterprises, 163-180.

Brown, Jennifer S. H. (1987). The Métis: Genesis and Rebirth. *Native People: Native Lands.* Bruce Alden Cox, ed. Ottawa, ON: Carleton University Press, 136-147.

Calihoo, Victoria. (1945). *Our Buffalo Hunt - 1874.* Edmonton, AB: Provincial Archives of Alberta. Unpublished manuscript, 4pp.

Campbell, Maria. (1973). *Halfbreed.* Toronto, ON: McClelland and Stewart.

Chalmers, John W. (1967). *Schools of the Foothills Province.* Toronto, ON: University of Toronto Press.

Chalmers, John W. (1972). *Education Behind the Buckskin Curtain.* Edmonton, AB: University of Alberta Press.

Chalmers, John W. (1974). Marguerite Bourgeoys: Preceptress of New France. *Profiles of Canadian Educators.* Robert S. Patterson, John W. Chalmers, and John W. Friesen, eds. Toronto, ON: D. C. Heath, 4-20.

Chalmers, John W. (1977). Schools for Our Other Indians: Education of Western Canadian Métis Children. *The Canadian West.* H. C. Klassen, ed. Calgary, AB: Comprint, 98-108.

Chalmers, John W. (1984). Northland: The Founding of a Wilderness School System. *Canadian Journal of Native Education. 12*:2, 2-45.

Charlebois, Peter. (1975). *The Life of Louis Riel.* Toronto, ON: New Canada Publications.

Clarke, Ann M., and A. D. B. Clarke. (1976). *Early Experience: Myth and Evidence.* New York: The Free Press.

Clarkson, Stephen & Christina McCall. (1990). *Trudeau and Our Times, Volume 1: The Magnificent Obsession.* Toronto, ON: McClelland and Stewart.

Coates, Ken. (Spring, 1990). Western Manitoba and the 1885 Rebellion. *Manitoba History, 19:* 32-41.

Cohen, J.M., and M.J. Cohen. (1985). *Dictionary of Quotations.* Middlesex, UK: Penguin.

Colombo, John Robert. (1987). *New Canadian Quotations.* Edmonton, AB: Hurtig Publishers.

Courchene, David. (1973). Problems and Possible Solutions. *Indians Without Tipis.* D. Bruce Sealey and Verna J. Kirkness, eds. Vancouver, BC: William Clare, 175-187.

Couture, Joseph E. (November, 1985). Traditional Native Thinking, Feeling, and Learning. *Multicultural Education Journal, 3*:2, 4-16.

Daniels, E. R. (May 23, 1967). A.S.T.A. Studies Possible Integration of Indian Students into Provincial Systems. *Alberta School Trustee, 37:* 23, 28.

Daniels, Harry W. (1979). *We Are the New Nation: The Métis and National Native Policy.* Ottawa, ON: Native Council of Canada.

Davidson, William McCartney. (1955). *Louis Riel, 1844-1885.* Calgary, AB: The Alberta Publishing Company.

de Tremaudan, A.H. (1982). *Hold High Your Heads: History of the Métis Nation in Western Canada.* Winnipeg, MB: Pemmican Publications.

DeFleur, Melvin L., William V. D'Antonio, & Louis B. DeFleur. (1973). *Sociology: Human Society.* Glenview, IL: Scott, Foresman & Co.

Dickason, Olive Patricia. (1984). *The Myth of the Savage and the Beginnings of French Colonialism in the Americas.* Edmonton, AB: University of Alberta Press.

Dickason, Olive Patricia. (1993). *Canada's First Nations: A History of Founding Peoples from Earliest Times.* Toronto, ON: McClelland and Stewart.

Dickason, Olive Patricia. (2001). From "One Nation" in the Northeast to "New Nation" in the Northwest: A Look at the Emergence of the Hmétis. *The New Peoples: Being and Becoming Métis in North America.* Fourth printing. Jacqueline Peterson and Jennifer S. H. Brown, eds. Winnipeg, MB: The University of Manitoba Press, 19-36.

Dobbin, Murray. (1981). *The One-and-a-Half Men: The Story of Jim Brady & Malcolm Norris, Métis Patriots of the 20th Century.* Vancouver, BC: New Star Books.

Dobbin, Murray. (nd). *An Introduction to Métis Social History.* Regina, SK: Gabriel Dumont Institute of Native Studies and Applied Research, 6 pp.

Dorion, Leah, and Darren R. Préfontaine. (2001). Deconstructing Métis Historiography: Giving Voice to the Métis People. *Métis Legacy: A Métis Historiography and Annotated Bibliography.* Lawrence J. Barkwell, Leah Dorion, and Darren Préfontaine, eds. Winnipeg, MB: Pemmican Publications, 13-36.

Driedger, Leo. (1989). *The Ethnic Factor: Identity in Diversity.* Toronto, ON: McGraw-Hill Ryerson.

Drouin, Emeric O., O.M.I. (Autumn, 1963). St. Paul des Métis. *Alberta Historical Review, 11*: 12-14.

Ens, Gerhard.(1983). Métis Lands in Manitoba. *Manitoba History,* 5:2-11.

Ens, Gerhard. (1988). Dispossession or Adaptation? Migration and Persistence of the Red River Métis, 1835-1890, *Canadian Historical Association Historical Papers,* 138-141.

Flanagan, Thomas. (1979a). *Louis 'David' Riel: Prophet of the New World.* Toronto, ON: University of Toronto Press.

Flanagan, Thomas. (1979b). *Louis Riel's Name 'David' Louis Riel and the Métis.* Antoine S. Lussier, ed. Winnipeg, MB: Pemmican Publications, 55-64.

Flanagan, Thomas. (1983). *Riel and the Rebellion: 1885 Reconsidered.* Saskatoon, SK: Western Producer Books.

Flanagan, Thomas. (1991a). *Métis Land Claims in Manitoba.* Calgary, AB: University of Calgary Press.

Flanagan, Thomas. (Spring, 1991b). The Market for Métis Lands in Manitoba: An Exploratory Study. *Prairie Forum, 16*:1, 1-20.

Foster, John E. (1979). The Métis: The People and the Term. *Louis Riel & the Métis* Antoine S. Lussier, ed. Winnipeg, MB: Pemmican Publications, 77-86.

Foster, John E. (2001). Some questions and perspectives on the problem of Métis roots. *Métis Legacy: A Métis Historiography and Annotated Bibliography.* Lawrence J. Barkwell, Leah Dorion, and Darren Pré-fontaine, eds. Winnipeg, MB: Pemmican Publications, 73-91.

Francis, R. Douglas, Richard Jones and Donald B. Smith. (1988). *Destinies: Canadian History Since Confederation.* Toronto, ON: Holt, Rinehart and Winston.

Frideres, James S., and René R. Gadacz. (2001). *Native Peoples in Canada: Contemporary Conflicts.* Sixth edition. Scarborough, ON: Prentice-Hall Canada.

Friesen, Gerald. (1984). *The Canadian Prairies: A History.* Toronto, ON: University of Toronto Press.

Friesen, John W. (1977). *People, Culture and Learning.* Calgary, AB: Detselig Enterprises.

Friesen, John W. (1983). *Schools with a Purpose.* Calgary, AB: Detselig Enterprises.

Friesen, John W. (1985). *When Cultures Clash: Case Studies in Multiculturalism.* Calgary, AB: Detselig Enterprises.

Friesen, John W. (1991a). Highlights of Western Canadian Native History. *The Cultural Maze: Complex Questions on Native Destiny in Western Canada.* John W. Friesen, ed. Calgary, AB: Detselig Enterprises, 1-22.

Friesen, John W. (1991b). Teaching in a University Native Outreach Program. *The Cultural Maze: Complex Questions on Native Destiny in Western Canada.* John W. Friesen, ed. Calgary, AB: Detselig Enterprises, 229-242.

Friesen, John W. (1991c). The Role of Native People in Canadian Multiculturalism.*The Cultural Maze: Complex Questions on Native Destiny in Western Canada.* John W. Friesen, ed. Calgary, AB: Detselig Enterprises, 243-256.

Friesen, John W. (1992). *Multiculturalism in Canada: Hope or Hoax?* Edmonton, AB: Alberta Teachers' Association.

Friesen, John W. (1995). *Pick One: A User-Friendly Guide to Religion.* Calgary, AB: Detselig Enterprises.

Friesen, John W. (1995). *You Can't Get There From Here: The Mystique of North American Plains Indians Culture & Philosophy.* Dubuque, IA: Kendall/Hunt.

Friesen, John W. (1996). *The Riel/Real Story: An Interpretive History of the Métis People of Canada*. Second edition. Ottawa, ON: Borealis Press.

Friesen, John W. (2000). *Aboriginal Theology and Biblical Theology: Closer Than You Think*. Calgary, AB: Detselig Enterprises.

Friesen, John W., and Alice L. Boberg. (1990). *Introduction to Teaching: A Socio-Cultural Approach*. Dubuque, IA: Kendall/Hunt.

Friesen, John W., and Virginia Lyons Friesen. (2002). *Aboriginal Education in Canada: A Plea for Integration*. Calgary, AB: Detselig Enterprises.

Friesen, John W., and Terry Lusty. (1980). *The Métis of Canada: An Annotated Bibliography*. Toronto, ON: The Ontario Institute for Studies in Education.

Frontier School Division No. 48. (2000). Winnipeg, MB: Province of Manitoba.

Fulham, S. (1972). *In Search of a Future*. Winnipeg, MB: Manitoba Métis-Federation Press.

Fumoleau, Rene. (1973). *As Long as This Land Shall Last: A History of Treaty 8 and Treaty 11, 1870-1939*. Toronto, ON: McClelland and Stewart.

Gaffney, R. E., G. P. Gould and A. J. Semple. (1984). *Broken Promises: The Aboriginal Constitutional Conferences*. St. Johns, NB: New Brunswick Association of Métis and Non-Status Indians.

Giraud, Marcel. (Winter, 1956). The Western Métis After the Insurrection, *Saskatchewan History*, IX:1, 1-15.

Giraud, Marcel. (1986). *The Métis in the Canadian West*. Two volumes. Translated by George Woodcock. Edmonton, AB: University of Alberta Press.

Gordon, Milton M. (1964). *Assimilation in American Life: The Role of Race, Religion and National Origins*. New York: Oxford University Press.

Hanrahan, Maura. (2000). Industrialization and the Politicalization of Health in Labrador Métis Society. *Canadian Journal of Native Studies*, XX:2, 231-250.

Hildebrandt, Walter. (1989). *The Battle of Batoche: British Small Warfare and the Entrenched Métis*. Ottawa, ON: Minister of Supply and Services.

House, Ernest R. (1992). Multicultural Evaluation in Canada and the United States, *The Canadian Journal of Program Evaluation*, 7:1, 133-156.

Howard, Joseph. (1974). *Strange Empire: Louis Riel and the Métis People*. Toronto, ON: James Lewis and Samuel.

Johnston, Darlene. (1989). *The Taking of Indian Lands in Canada: Consent or Coercion?* Saskatoon, SK: University of Saskatchewan Native Law Centre.

Kirkness, Verna J. (1973). In Pursuit of Honour and Justice. *Indians Without Tipis,* D. Bruce Sealey and Verna J. Kirkness, eds. Vancouver, BC: William Clare, 205-214.

Knill, William D., and Arthur K. Davies. (1966). Provincial Education in Northern Saskatchewan: Progress and Bog-Down, 144-162. *A Northern Dilemma: Reference Papers,* Vol. 1, Arthur K. Davies, ed. Bellingham, WA: Western Washington State College, 170-337.

Knox, Olive. (1978). The Question of Louis Riel's Insanity. *The Other Natives: the-les Métis, Volume One, 1700-1885.* Antoine S. Lussier and D. Bruce Sealey, eds. Winnipeg. MB: Manitoba Métis Federation Press, 205-224.

Knudtson, Peter, and David Suzuki. (1992). *Wisdom of the Elders.* Toronto, ON: Stoddart Publishing Company.

Lagasse, Jean H., dir. (1959). *A Study of the Population of Indian Ancestry Living in Manitoba.* Three Volumes. Winnipeg, MB: Department of Agriculture and Immigration.

Lalonde, Andre N. (Autumn, 1974). The North-West Rebellion and Its Effects on Settlers and Settlement in the Canadian West. *Saskatchewan History,* 27:3, 95-102.

Lang, H. R., and D. R. Scarfe. (1985). *The Group as Support in a Native Teacher Education Program.* Montreal, PQ: The Canadian Association of Teacher Educators, Canadian Society for the Study of Education.

LaRoque, Emma. (1975). *Defeathering the Indian.* Agincourt, ON: The Book Society of Canada.

Ledgerwood, C. D. (1972). *Native Education in the Province of Alberta.* Edmonton, AB: Minister of Education, Government of Alberta.

Li, Peter S. (1988). *Ethnic Inequality in a Class Society.* Toronto, ON: Thompson Educational Publishing.

Lower, Arthur R. M. (1977). *Colony to Nation: A History of Canada.* Toronto, ON: McClelland and Stewart.

Lussier, Antoine S. (1979). *Louis Riel & the Métis.* Winnipeg, MB: Pemmican Publications.

Lussier, Antoine S. (1982). Introduction. *Hold High Your Heads: History of the Métis Nation in Western Canada.* A.-H. de Tremaudan, ed. Winnipeg, MB: Pemmican Publications.

Lussier, Antoine S. and D. Bruce Sealey. (1978). *The Other Natives: the-les Métis.Volume One: 1700-1885: Volume Two: 1885-1978,* Winnipeg, MB: Manitoba Métis Federation Press.

Lusty, Terrance. (1973). *Louis Riel: Humanitarian.* Calgary, AB: Printing Co.

MacEwan, Grant. (1981). *Métis Makers of History.* Saskatoon, SK: Western Producer Books.

MacEwan, Grant. (1995). *Buffalo: Sacred & Sacrificed.* Edmonton, AB: Alberta Sport, Recreation, Parks and Wildlife.

MacNeil, Harold, Chair. (1981). *Report of the Northland School Division Investigation Committee.* Edmonton, AB: Department of Education.

Mailhot, P. R., and D. N. Sprague. (1985). Persistent Settlers: The Dispersal and Resettlement of the Red River Métis, 1870-1885. *Canadian Ethnic Studies,* XVII:2, 1-30.

Manitoba MétisFederation. (1978). *Riverlots and Scrip: Elements of Métis Aboriginal Rights.* Winnipeg, MB: Manitoba Métis Federation Press.

Mattes, Catherine. (2001). Métis Perspectives in Contemporary Art. *Métis Legacy: A Métis Historiography and Annotated Bibliography.* Lawrence J. Barkwell, Leah Dorion, and Darren Préfontaine, eds. Winnipeg, MB: Pemmican Publications, 189-192.

McDonald, N. G. (1974). David J. Goggin, Promoter of National Schools. *Profiles of Canadian Educators.* Robert S. Patterson, John W. Chalmers, and John W. Friesen, eds. Toronto, ON: D.C. Heath, 167-185.

McHugh, Tom. (1972). *The Time of the Buffalo.* Lincoln, NE: University of Nebraska Press.

McLean, Don. (1985). *1885: Métis Rebellion or Government Conspiracy?* Winnipeg, MB: Pemmican Publications.

McLean, Don. (1987). *Fifty Historical Vignettes: Views of the Common People.* Regina, SK: Gabriel Dumont Institute of Métis Studies and Applied Research.

McLean, Don. (1988). *Home From the Hill: A History of the Métis in Western Canada.* Regina, SK: Gabriel Dumont Institute of Métis Studies and Applied Research.

MétisAssociation of Alberta, and Joe Sawchuk, Patricia Sawchuk and Theresa Ferguson. (1981). *Métis Lands in Alberta: A Political History.* Edmonton, AB: Métis Association of Alberta.

Moodley, Kogila A. (1992). Ethnicity, Power, Politics and Minority Education. *Beyond Multicultural Education: International Perspectives.* Kogila A. Moodley, ed. Calgary, AB: Detselig Enterprises, 79-94.

Morgan, Patricia. (1975). *Child Care: Sense or Fable.* London, UK: Temple Smith.

Morton, Arthur S. (1939). *The New Nation: The Métis. Proceedings and Transactions of the Royal Society of Canada.* Series 3, Section 2, 33: 137-145.

Morton, W. L. (September, 1950). The Canadian Métis. *The Beaver, 281*: 3-7.

Mulvaney, Charles Pelham. (1885). *The History of the North-West Rebellion of 1885.* Toronto, ON: A. H. Hovey and Co. Reprinted in 1971 by Coles Publishing Company of Toronto, Ontario.

Nicks, Trudy. (1985). Mary Anne's Dilemma: The Ethnohistory of an Ambivalent Identity, *Canadian Ethnic Studies,* XVII:2, 103-114.

Nicks, Trudy, and Kenneth Morgan. (2001). Grande Cache: The historic development of an indigenous Alberta Métis Population. *Métis Legacy: A Métis Historiography and Annotated Bibliography.* Lawrence J. Barkwell, Leah Dorion, and Darren Préfontaine, eds. Winnipeg, MB: Pemmican Publications, 163-181.

Palmer, Howard, with Tamara Palmer. (1990). *Alberta: A History.* Edmonton, AB: Hurtig Publishers.

Pannekoek, Fritz. (1979). Some Comments on the Social Origins of the Riel Protest of 1869. *Louis Riel & the Métis.* Antoine S. Lussier, ed. Winnipeg, MB: Pemmican Publications, 65-76.

Patterson, E. Palmer II. (1972). *The Canadian Indian: A History Since 1500.* Don Mills, ON: Collier-Macmillan Canada.

Patterson, Robert S., John W. Chalmers, and John W. Friesen, eds. (1974). *Profiles of Canadian Educators.* Toronto, ON: D.C. Heath.

Payment, Diane Paulette. (1990)."*The Free People–Otipemisiwak:" Batoche, Saskatchewan, 1870-1930s.* Ottawa, ON: National Historic Parks and Sites, Parks Service.

Pelletier, Emile. (1977). *A Social History of the Manitoba Métis.* Winnipeg, MB: Manitoba Métis Federation Press.

Peters, Evelyn, Mark Rosenberg, and Greg Halseth. (1991). The Ontario Métis : Some Aspects of a Métis Identity. Canadian *Ethnic Studies,* XXIII:l, 71-84.

Peterson, Jacqueline, and Jennifer S. H. Brown, eds. (1985). *The New Peoples: Being and Becoming Métis in North America.* Fourth printing. Winnipeg, MB: The University of Manitoba Press.

Peterson, Jacqueline, and Jennifer S. H. Brown. (2001). Introduction. *The New Peoples: Being and Becoming Métis in North America.* Jacqueline Peterson and Jennifer S. H. Brown, eds. Fourth printing. Winnipeg, MB: The University of Manitoba Press, 3-16.

Pockington, T C. (1991). *The Government and the Politics of the Alberta Métis Settlements.* Regina, SK: Canadian Plains Research Center, University of Regina.

Purich, Donald. (1988). *The Métis .* Toronto, ON: James Lorimer.

Racette, Sherry Farrell. (2001). Beads, Silk and Quills: The Clothing and Decorative Arts of the Métis . *Métis Legacy: A Métis Historiography and Annotated Bibliography.* Lawrence J. Barkwell, Leah Dorion, and Darren Préfontaine, eds. Winnipeg, MB: Pemmican Publications, 181-188.

Ray, Arthur. (2002). When Two Worlds Met. *The Illustrated History of Canada.* Craig Brown, ed., Toronto, ON: Key Porter Books, 1-94.

Redbird, Duke. (*1980).We Are Métis : A Métis View of the Development of a Native Canadian People.* Willowdale, ON: Ontario Métis & Non-Status Association.

Roberts, Lance, Susanne von Below, and Mathias Bos. (2001). The Métis in a Multicultural Society: Some Reflections on the Macro Picture. *Métis Legacy: A Métis Historiography and Annotated Bibliography.* Lawrence J. Barkwell, Leah Dorion, and Darren R. Préfontaine, eds. Winnipeg, MB: Pemmican Publications, 193-198.

Robertson, Heather. (August, 1970). On the Road to Nowhere. *Saturday Night, 85*:8, 17-22.

Robertson, Heather. (March/April, 1992). The Forks, Manitoba: Shaking the Spirit of Louis Riel. *Equinox, 62*: 83-102.

Sargent, S.S. (1949). *Culture and Personality.* New York: The Viking Fund.

Scott-Brown, Joan. (1991) Native Land Claims. *The Cultural Maze: Complex Questions on Native Destiny in Western Canada.* John W. Friesen, ed. Calgary, AB: Detselig Enterprises, 97-110.

Sealey, D. Bruce. (1977). The Métis : Schools, Identity and Conflict. *Canadian Schools and Canadian Identity.* Alf Chaiton and Neil McDonald, eds. Toronto, ON: Gage Educational Publishing, 150-164

Sealey, D. Bruce. (1980). *The Education of Native Peoples in Manitoba. Monographs in Education,* No. III, Winnipeg. MB: University of Manitoba.

Sealey, D. Bruce, and Verna J. Kirkness. (1973). *Indians Without Tipis: A Resource Book by Indians and Métis* . Vancouver, BC: William Clare.

Sealey, D. Bruce, and Antoine S. Lussier. (1975). *The Métis: Canada's Forgotten People.* Winnipeg, MB: Manitoba MétisFederation Press.

Shaw, George Bernard. (1985). *The Revolutionist's Handbook. Dictionary of Quotations.* J.M. Cohen and M.J. Cohen, eds. New York: Penguin Books.

Shilstone, Arthur. (January, 1992). Europe's First Foothold in the New World. *National Geographic, 181*:1, 41-51.

Shore, Fred J. (2001). The Emergence of the Métis Nation in Manitoba. *Métis Legacy: A Métis Historiography and Annotated Bibliography.* Lawrence J. Barkwell, Leah Dorion, and Darren Préfontaine, eds. Winnipeg, MB: Pemmican Publications, 71-78.

Shore, Fred J., and Lawrence J. Barkwell. (1997). *Past Reflects the Present: The Métis Elders' Conference.* Winnipeg, MB: Manitoba Métis Federation.

Siggins, Maggie. (1994). *Riel: A Life of Revolution.* Toronto, ON: Harper-Collins.

Slobodin, Richard. (1963). *Métis of the Mackenzie District.* Ottawa, ON: Canadian Research Centre for Anthropology.

Smith, Donald B. (Spring, 1981). William Henry Jackson: Riel's Secretary. *The Beaver, 311*:4, 10-19.

Smith, Donald B. (1985). The Original Peoples of Alberta. *Peoples of Alberta: Portraits of Cultural Diversity.* Howard and Tamara Palmer, eds. Saskatoon, SK: Western Producer Books, 50-83.

Spinard, Leonard and Thelma. (1987). *Speaker's Lifetime Library.* Volume 4. West Nyack, NY: Parker Publishing Co.

Sprague, D. N. (1988). *Canada and the Métis, 1869-1885.* Waterloo, ON:Wilfred Laurier University Press.

Sprague, D. N. (Fall, 1991). Dispossession vs. Accommodation in Plaintiff vs. Defendant Accounts of Métis Dispersal from Manitoba, 1870-1881. *Prairie Forum, 16*:2, 137-156.

Sprenger, G. Herman. (1978). The Métis Nation: Buffalo Hunting vs. Agriculture in the Red Riel Settlement. *The Other Natives: the-les Métis,*

Volume One, 1700-1885. Antoine S. Lussier and D. Bruce Sealey, eds. Winnipeg, MB: Manitoba Métis Federation Press, 115-130.

Spry, Irene. (2001). The Métis and Mixed-Bloods of Rupert's Land Before 1870. *The New Peoples: Being and Becoming Métis in North America.* Jacqueline Peterson and Jennifer S. H. Brown, eds. Fourth printing. Winnipeg, MB: The University of Manitoba Press, 95-118.

Stanley, George F. G. (1960). *The Birth of Western Canada: A History of the Riel Rebellions.* Toronto, ON: University of Toronto Press.

Stanley, George F. G. (1963). *Louis Riel.* Toronto, ON: Ryerson Press.

Stanley, George F. G. (1970). *Louis Riel, Patriot or Rebel. Historical Booklet, No. 2,* Ottawa, ON: Canadian Historical Association.

Stanley, George F. G. (1978). Louis Riel: Patriot or Rebel? *The Other Natives: the-les Métis, Volume One, 1700-1885.* Antoine S. Lussier and D. Bruce Sealey, eds. Winnipeg, MB: Manitoba Métis Federation Press, 177-204.

Statistics Canada. (2003). *2001 Census: Analysis Series. Aboriginal Peoples of Canada: A Demographic Profile.* Ottawa, ON: Minister of Supply and Services, Catalogue No. 96F0030XIE2001007.

Stock, Brian. (May 14, 1976). The Vicissitudes of Nationalism. The Times Literary Supplement. *New Canadian Quotations,* John Robert Colombo, ed. Edmonton, AB: Hurtig Publishers, 1987.

Tobias, J. L. (1988). Indian Reserves in Western Canada: Indian Homelands or Devices for Assimilation? *Native People: Native Lands.* Bruce Alden Cox, ed. Ottawa, ON: Carleton University Press, 148-157.

van den Berghe, Pierre L. (1981). *The Ethnic Phenomenon.* New York: Elsevier.

Verrall, Catherine, and Lenore Keeshig-Tobias. (1987). *Annotated Bibliography of Resources By and About Native People.* Toronto, ON: Canadian Alliance in Solidarity with the Native Peoples.

Waite, Peter. (2002). Between Three Oceans: Challenges of a Continental Destiny *(1840-1900). The Illustrated History of Canada.* Toronto, ON: Key Porter Books. 277-376.

Weaver, Sally M. (1985). Federal Policy-Making for Métis and Non-Status Indians in the Context of Native Policy. Canadian *Ethnic Studies,* XVII:2, 80-102.

Whidden, Lynn. (2001). Métis Music. *Métis Legacy: A Métis Historiography and Annotated Bibliography.* Lawrence J. Barkwell, Leah Dorion, and Darren R. Préfontaine, eds. Winnipeg, MB: Pemmican Publications, 169-176.

Williams, Glyndwr, (Autumn, 1983). The Hudson's Bay Company and the Fur Trade: 1670-1870, *The Beaver,* 314:2, 1-81.

Woodcock, George. (1976). *Gabriel Dumont: The Métis Chief and His Lost World.* Edmonton, AB: Hurtig Publishers.

Young, Kimball. (1944). *Social Psychology.* New York: Appleton-Century-Crofts

About the Authors

John W. Friesen, Ph.D., D.Min., D.R.S., a native of Duck Lake SK, is a Professor in the Faculty of Education and the Faculty of Communication and Culture at the University of Calgary where he teaches courses and conducts research in Aboriginal history and education. He is the author of more than 40 books including:

The Métis of Canada: An Annotated Bibliography (co-editor) (OISE, 1980);

Rose of the North (Borealis, 1987);

You Can't Get There From Here: The Mystique of North American Plains Indians Culture & Philosophy (Kendall/Hunt, 1995);

The Riel/Real Story: An Interpretive History of the Métis People of Canada, second edition (Borealis, 1996);

The Community Doukhobors: A People in Transition (co-author) (Borealis, 1996);

Rediscovering the First Nations of Canada (Detselig, 1997);

First Nations of the Plains: Creative, Adaptable and Enduring (Detselig, 1999);

Aboriginal Spirituality and Biblical Theology: Closer Than You Think, (Detselig, 2000);

Do Christians Forgive? Well, Some Do... (Borealis, 2000);

Aboriginal Education in Canada: A Plea for Integration (co-author) (Detselig, 2002); and,

Canadian Society in the Twenty-First Century: An Historical Sociological Approach (co-author), (Pearson Canada, 2004).

Virginia Lyons Friesen, Ph.D., is a Sessional Instructor in the Faculty of Communication and Culture at the University of Calgary where she teaches courses in Canadian culture and Aboriginal education. She is a specialist in Early Childhood

Education, and holds a Certificate in Counseling from the Institute of Pastoral Counseling in Akron, Ohio.

She has co-presented a number of papers at academic conferences, and co-authored several books including:

Grade Expectations: A Multicultural Handbook for Teachers, (Alberta Teachers' Association, 1995),

In Defense of Public Schools in North America (Detselig, 2001);

Aboriginal Education in Canada: A Plea for Integration (Detselig, 2002); and,

The Palgrave Companion to Utopian Communities in North America (Palgrave Macmillan, 2004).

Index

Adams, Howard, 45-46, 118, 121, 133

Alberta, 12, 16, 17, 18, 28, 62, 108, 118, 119, 120

Alberta Federation of Métis Settlements, 41, 42, 110

Alberta Métis Association, 25

annual buffalo hunt, 58f

Association of Métis and non-Status Indans of Saskatchewan, 144

Batoche, 10, 87, 90, 92-93

Battle of Seven Oaks, 42, 66, 139

Belcourt, Tony, 24

Bellhumeur, Marguerite, 85

Benedict, Ruth, 31-32

Bennett, Prime Minister R.B., 11

Berger, Thomas R., 11

Blackfoot Confederacy, 53

Blais, Ernest, 4

bloodlines, 8, 11, 18, 24, 25, 41, 43, 142

Brandon University, 134

British North America Act, 49

buffalo bones, 62-63

buffalo hunting, 60f

buffalo jump, 60

buffalo pound, 59

Cabot, John (Giovanni Caboto), 13

Callihoo, Victoria, 59

Campbell, Maria, 35, 45, 117

Camperville, MB, 130-132

Canadian Census, 9

Canadian Charter of Rights and Freedoms, 112

Canadian Pacific Railway, 49

Cartier, Jacques, 13

Charter Nation, 23

Chipewyan, 17

civil rights movement, 27

Civil War, 102

Congress of Aboriginal Peoples, 71, 109, 110

Couture, Joseph, 50

Cree(s), 43, 52, 53, 54

Creighton, Donald, 37

cultural, culture, customs, 8, 9, 25, 26, 32-34, 39, 51, 57, 64, 71, 98, 108, 115, 139, 140, 145

de Tremaudan, Auguste-Henri, 35-36

Dickason, Olive, 13

Dominion Lands Act, 44

doublebreed, 41

Douglas, Thomas, Earl of Selkirk, 64

Douglas, T.C., 108

Duck Lake, 10

Dumont, Gabriel, 85, 86, 87, 88

Dumont, Isidore, 86

Edmonton, 12, 38

elders, 25

embroidery, 57

Ens, Gerhard, 38, 49

Ewing Commission, 106

flag(s), 29

Flanagan, Thomas, 16-17, 37, 38, 49, 50

Fort Chipewyan, AB, 126-130

fraud, 100, 101

Fremont, Donatien, 36

Frontier School Division, 125

Gaboury, Marie-Anne, 75

Gabriel Dumont Insitute, 8, 101, 116, 134

Gladue, Trevor, 24
Goggin, David J., 140-141
Goodale, Ralph, 24
Goyette, Linda, 38
Grant, Cuthbert, 65, 139
Grant, Ulysses Simpson, 83
Guernon, Marie-Julie, 74, 77

Haida, 31
halfbreed(s), half-breed(s), breed(s), 15, 35, 41, 57, 99, 100, 103
Haultain, F.W., 140
historiography, 34f
Hudson's Bay, Hudson's Bay Company, 15, 16, 37, 52, 53, 54, 65, 66, 69, 70, 75, 79, 80, 139
Human Rights Commission, 131-132
Hutterite, 123

Indian Act, 19, 107, 142
Indian Association of Alberta, 142
Inuit, 10, 43

Jackson, William Henry, 16

Kelsey, Henry, 53
King Charles II, 53

Labrador, 43
Lacombe, Albert, 103-104, 105
Lagimodiére, Jean-Baptiste, 75
Lagimodiére, Julie, 17, 75, 76
language, 14-15, 19, 44, 57
Laurier, William, 17, 74
Lougheed, Peter, 17, 112
Louis Riel Institute, 7, 116
Lussier, Antoine, 45, 46, 133

Macdonald, John A., 16, 49, 82-83
Macdonell, Alexander, 65
Macdonall, Miles, 64, 65
MacNeil Commission, 127-128, 129

Manitoba, 12, 28, 30, 42, 48, 49, 56, 59, 93-95, 100, 101, 102, 108, 123-125, 131
Manitoba Act of 1870, 49-50, 91, 97, 112
Manitoba Appeal Court, 50
Manitoba Métis Federation, 7, 8, 38, 45, 48, 109, 115, 116, 126, 134, 144
McDougall, William, 80, 81
Métis Association of Alberta, 16, 101, 118
Métis Betterment Act, 18
Métis colonies, 106-108
Métis identity, 41f
Métis land claims, 39, 49
Métis Nation of Alberta, 24
Métis National Council, 38, 44, 71, 110, 113
Métis Population Betterment Act, 106
Michif, 25, 57
Micmac, 43
Middleton, Frederick Dobson, 87-88
Montana, 20, 102
Morice, Father A.G., 36
Morton, W.L., 37
multicultural, 51, 57, 139

National Committee of the Métis of Red River, 70, 80, 81, 82
Native Council of Canada, 47, 109, 112
Necolonialism, 142
Newfoundland, 43
nonstatus, 41, 47, 48, 107, 142, 143
North West Company, 53, 56, 65
North West Trading Company, 54, 67
Northcote, 89
Northern Lights School Division, 121

Northland School Division, 108, 122-123, 125, 128
Northland School Division Act, 130
Nova Scotia, 42

Ojibway, 17, 43, 52, 54
Oliver, Frank, 104
Ontario, 6, 28, 55, 84
Ontario Métis and Non-Status Association, 44, 109
Order-in-Council, 99, 103

pemmican, 62
Powell, John Wesley, 14
Powler, Roddy, 6
Powley, Steve, 6
prenuptial agreement, 78

Red River, MB, 42, 44, 48, 55, 56, 58-59, 62, 67, 68, 75, 79
Red River Cart, 5, 59, 62, 63
Red River Jig, 25, 57, 58
Reel, Jean Baptiste, 17
residential schools, 19
Riel, Louis, 15, 16, 17, 18, 19, 23, 27-28, 30, 32, 37, 70, 73, 90-91, 93 134, 143, 144
Riel, Louis David, 15, 74
Riel, Louis Sr., 17, 74, 75-76, 77
Riel's birth, 74
Riel's death, 73
Riel's defeat, 97
Riel's expulsion, 84
Riel's marriage, 75
Riel's poetry, 58
Riel Rebellion(s), 34, 36, 98
Roman Catholic, Roman Catholic Church, 25, 32, 36, 38
Royal Commission on Aboriginal People, 9
Royal Proclamation of 1763, 37, 112, 113
running the herd, 59

Rupert's Land, 53, 80

St. Paul des Métis Colony, 103-108
St. Marie, Buffy, 41
Saskatchewan, 28, 47, 62, 85, 108, 109, 118, 119, 120-121, 133
Saskatchewan Urban Teacher Education Program, 134
Sayer incident, 76
school(s), 18, 38, 42, 108, 116, 117, 120, 137
School Attendance Act, 119
Scott, Thomas, 82, 84
scrip, 26, 38-39, 85, 98-101
Sealey, D. Bruce, 45, 46, 133
self-image, 34
Semple, Robert, 66
Seven Oaks, 66
Sifton, Clifford, 104
Simpson, George, 68, 69
Sneakup, 62
Snow, John A., 79, 81
Spry, Irene, 49
speculators, 101
Status, Status Indians, 9, 10, 19, 23, 26, 28, 35, 43, 86, 98, 107, 111, 116, 118, 140, 142, 143
Supreme Court, Supreme Court of Canada, 6, 24, 25, 29, 42, 46, 112, 113, 137

Tache, Alexandre, 76, 77, 93
Therien, Josephy-Adeodat, 103, 105
Tough, Frank, 38
Treaty, treaties, 26, 38, 111, 142, 143
Tripartite Cooperative Agreement, 138

Union Nationale Métisse, 36
United Nations Assembly, 30
University of Calgary Native Outreach Program, 128, 134
University of Saskatchewan, 134

Vaillancourt, Judge Charles, 6-7
War of 1812, 66
Winnipeg, 10, 12, 55, 68
Wolseley, Garnet, 83
Woodland Cree(s), 17, 52
World War I, 31
World War II, 119